Praise for Andy Grove

"Perhaps the key executive in America's key industry, Mr. Grove demonstrates his grasp of all the complexities of running a business of human beings."
—*The Wall Street Journal*

"*One-on-One With Andy Grove* is fun. He makes a lot of good points but the reader ends up the winner. His advice to a mother returning to work after raising a family is simply vintage Andy Grove—look out, Abby."
—Rand V. Araskog, Chairman and CEO of ITT Corp.

"Andrew S. Grove is at the center of the confrontation in high technology between his innovative company, the Intel Corporation, and some of Japan's most powerful trading companies."
—*The New York Times*

"Grove approaches confrontation as a connoisseur. He puts all the intensity of his personality behind his analysis and refuses to accept anything less than well—thought-out, unembellished answers."
—*Fortune*

PENGUIN BOOKS

ONE-ON-ONE WITH ANDY GROVE

Andrew S. Grove is the president and chief executive officer of Intel Corporation and author of the classic *High Output Management*. He lives in California.

One-on-One
With
Andy Grove

HOW TO MANAGE YOUR BOSS, YOURSELF, AND YOUR COWORKERS

ANDREW S. GROVE

Penguin Books

PENGUIN BOOKS
Published by the Penguin Group
Viking Penguin Inc., 40 West 23rd Street,
New York, New York 10010, U.S.A.
Penguin Books Ltd, 27 Wrights Lane,
London W8 5TZ, England
Penguin Books Australia Ltd, Ringwood,
Victoria, Australia
Penguin Books Canada Ltd, 2801 John Street,
Markham, Ontario, Canada L3R 1B4
Penguin Books (N.Z.) Ltd, 182–190 Wairau Road,
Auckland 10, New Zealand

Penguin Books Ltd, Registered Offices:
Harmondsworth, Middlesex, England

First published in the United States of America by
G. P. Putnam's Sons 1987
Published in Penguin Books 1988

LIBRARY OF CONGRESS CATALOGING IN PUBLICATION DATA
Grove, Andrew S.
  One-on-one with Andy Grove.
  Originally published: New York: G. P. Putnam's Sons,
c1987.
  1. Managing your boss.   2. Interpersonal relations.
3. Personnel management.   I. Title.
HF5548.83.G77   1988   650.1'3   88-5869
ISBN 0 14 01.0935 8

Printed in the United States of America by
R. R. Donnelley & Sons Company, Harrisonburg, Virginia
Set in Times Roman

THANKS . . .

. . . are due to the editors of the *San Jose Mercury News*, who recognized that there are many people out there with questions about how to manage at the workplace. Thanks also to readers of that newspaper and others elsewhere in the U.S. who thought that I might have answers.

I am grateful to Karen Thorpe for helping me with the seemingly never-ending task of putting this book together, always maintaining an even temper, even when I lost mine. But, most of all, I am indebted to my wife, Eva. Through countless "one-on-ones," she did her best to make sure that my advice was practical, my prose readable, and that I dealt with the questions that were posed and not the ones I wished had been. There probably has never been a muse more constructively critical of her subject!

Contents

Contents

Your Breath After Meetings • A Secretary Needs a Boss's
Time • Too Much of a Good Thing—at Work, Too • Write
Notes to Yourself—So You Won't Forget • Instant Action Can
Cure Procrastination

Contents

Introduction:
Everybody Is a Manager!

I have been a manager for over twenty years. I've managed small groups and big departments. I had successes and I had failures. I enjoyed myself, and I fretted. I taught hundreds of coworkers and I also learned much from them.

As president of Intel Corporation, a microchip manufacturer employing over 18,000 people around the world, I am often asked to speak on the subject of managing. My talks are usually followed by a question-and-answer session, after which people also come up to ask my opinion about problems they have at work. The great variety of such problems intrigued me, and so when the San Jose Mercury News offered me the opportunity to write a weekly question-and-answer column on the subject of managing, I jumped at the chance.

Writing the column exposed me to an even broader range of work problems. People who would never think of attending my talks wrote and solicited my advice or reaction to situations they faced at work. All kinds of people wrote: store clerks, owners of small companies, college students, department managers at large organizations—people from just about every conceivable work situation.

As I kept reading and answering questions from the work-lorn and the work-worn, I couldn't overlook the fact that the overwhelming majority of writers asked for help with interpersonal relationships at work. People wanted ideas on how to deal with the boss who never gives feedback, with the employee who doesn't care about her work, with the customer who propositions them, with coworkers who steal or who crack their gum loudly. In other words, people wanted ideas on how to *manage* better at their workplace: manage as in "the boss manages his employees," and also manage as in "make do" or "get along."

I decided that there was a real need for a book about *managing* that addressed both meanings. As I see it, everybody is a manager. The oldest and most frequently used definition of the word is "getting things done through other people." Getting along at the work place also requires exactly that: getting things done yourself or through your employees, your peers, and most important of all, your own boss. So, everybody who works *is* indeed a manager whether or not he or she holds that title.

Twenty-some years ago I would not have thought I'd ever find myself in a position of giving such advice. I certainly didn't start my career with any notions of ever becoming a manager in any sense of the word. When I was in my early twenties, a close friend asked if I wanted to get into management. I looked at him in amazement, wondering if he had lost his marbles, and answered that I just couldn't see wasting my time that way. So, how did it all happen? As I now look back, I realize that there were several incidents that, each in their own way, nudged me to where I am today.

The first took place in Hungary, where I was born. I was fourteen years old and I aspired to become a journalist. I wrote with ease, enjoyed it, and was a reporter for the youth newspaper. Like everything else in Communist Hungary, this paper was under the influence of the regime. I wrote about nonpolitical student concerns, like going back to school after summer vacation, making friends, and the like. Most everything I wrote was published in the paper, and I was enthusiastic and happy.

Some time later, a relative fell into disfavor and was imprisoned without trial—not an uncommon occurrence in Hungary during those years. After that none of my articles saw print.

Being a naive kid, I didn't see the connection between these two events for quite a while. Later it dawned on me that I was also getting a cold shoulder from the people who ran the newspaper. Not only did they not print my pieces, they even stopped talking to me.

I was as crushed as only a slighted adolescent can be. Eventually my depression gave way to the determination never to find myself in that kind of a situation again. I did not want a profession in which a totally subjective evaluation, easily colored by political considerations, could decide the merits of my work. I ran from writing to science.

Next, a very special night on a train comes to mind. It was taking several hundred Hungarian refugees, myself included, who had left the country in the aftermath of the 1956 uprising from Vienna to the German port city of Bremerhaven. There a ship bound for the U.S. was waiting for us. On the train I stared out the window at the dark countryside racing by, deep in thought. The reality of leaving the country of my birth for a faraway and unknown land was sinking into my twenty-year-old consciousness. Even as I was enveloped by the fear of the many unknowns in my future, I began to realize that I would no longer have to pretend to believe in things that I detested just to get by.

I settled in New York and started to study engineering at the City College of New York. In my first year, as a refugee, I received a scholarship. When it ran out, I sought help from the chairman of my department. He was a crusty old guy; even macho seniors trembled at the sight of him. I sat in his office, need having overcome my hesitancy to approach him. He looked at me with those famous piercing eyes as I told him my hard-luck story. Hungarian refugees were still in the news, and frankly I hoped that would help me get another scholarship.

The piercing eyes waited until I finished my story. Then he asked how much I needed to live on. I told him. He whipped out the longest slide rule I have ever seen, calculated for a while, and looked at me again. He asked, "How about working for it, young man? You could earn what you need in twenty hours of work a week. It will do you good." So I ended up working for crusty Professor Schmidt, running his copies and his errands, typing with two fingers, filing, whatever—and supported myself through my remaining years of college that way. It did do me good, in more ways than one. Day in and day out I was exposed to Professor Schmidt's blunt, no-nonsense, results-oriented yet caring personality. I like to think that some of it rubbed off on me.

A few years later, armed with a Ph.D., I started work at Fairchild Semiconductor, the then-leading Silicon Valley chip-research laboratory. I was a member of a small research group. My assignment was to come up with explanations—theories, if you like—that made sense out of the experimental findings of my coworkers. Once such theories existed, they would provide ideas for other experiments. As the "theorist" of our group, I found myself giving direction to my colleagues. I wasn't their boss, yet I influenced their work and activities. Later I was promoted and became the head of this same group. Now I could give direction by virtue of my new position. Yet there was no change in the relationship between me and the other members of the group. I discovered that it was "knowledge power" more than "position power" that enabled me to influence the activities of others, to manage.

There is a real distinction between the two, and this became even clearer to me in the early days of Intel. Here I started out with a nice sounding title—director of operations. The trouble was, I knew very little about the work some of my subordinates were doing. One was a manufacturing expert, another a computer-memory designer. In my previous research position I had no exposure to either field. Even so, I was, in name at least, responsible for their work. What to do? Simple. I arranged for "private lessons" with each. Several times a week I sat down with one or the other, notepaper in hand, and got on with my next lesson in manufacturing or memory design. After a long series of lessons, I became conversant enough to listen to them more intelligently and gradually even to offer some reasonable suggestions. Another key lesson in my development as a manager had taken place: the importance of learning from one's employees.

Seven or eight years later I was put in charge of the operations of the rest of the company and again found myself responsible for activities with which I had no previous experience. I went through the exact same process: I had my new subordinates (this time they were division general managers) give me tutorials on the basics of their businesses.

The early years at Intel left a huge impression on me in another way as well. In those days, even as the company fought to get started in business, there was a whole lot of jockeying for position. In time it became clear to me that the situation was much like people in a lifeboat crowding to the bow instead of helping to row the boat along—as if anyone could get to safety faster by being up front! Those hard, stressful years (everything matters so much when you are struggling to get a company off the ground) taught me an excruciatingly painful lesson about the importance of teamwork.

As Intel grew, we developed a style of management with which my old professor at City College would have felt right at home: straightforward, blunt, no-nonsense, results-oriented. We started on the road to becoming an international company and opened factories and offices in faraway countries. One day I was getting ready for my first trip to the Far East to help start a new facility there. Never having been there before, I sought help, and the most important advice I got was: "Andy, don't be your usual self! People over there are not used to bluntness; diplomatic and circumspect behavior is a must!"

I left with the best of intentions. When I sat with our managers in our new Malaysian plant, listening to a litany of problems the group was trying to cope with, I was indeed very polite. I smiled a lot and nodded my head even as I was wringing my hands under the table. The solutions were staring these managers in the face, I thought, but they were going around in circles. Eventually I couldn't contain myself. I exclaimed, "Look, you are all missing the point!" and elucidated my own views in the most straightforward of terms. A moment of silence greeted my comments, along with some awkward looks. Then, one by one, the Malaysian managers joined in the discussion, and, notwithstanding that plain talk was supposed to be unacceptable in the Orient, the meeting turned into an energetic problem-solving session. Incidents like this have convinced me that people are basically the same everywhere and that catering to stereotypical notions of interpersonal styles is nothing short of condescension. Straightforwardness always works best.

In the last few years, relentless global competitors hammered away at us, challenging every bit of managerial skill that I accumulated in over twenty years of managing. In this period rapid business growth in one year was followed by contraction in the next; there were times when we asked our employees to work an extra 25 percent, followed by others when we had to cut their pay. In short, it's been like a roller-coaster ride. These years reinforced my belief that if you want your employees to follow you through the gyrations of your business, you must make sure that they have access to the same facts and perspectives that you do.

Intel has always been an open company, with strong flow of information up, down, and sideways. In this tough period that tradition turned out to be exceedingly valuable. And while you may nod your head in easy agreement that yes, of course, communication is good, don't think for a moment that it's easy. True communication means facing concerns head-on, and that can be very hard, particularly when times are tough.

At Intel we have a tradition of conducting a type of meeting we call "Open Forums." At these, a senior manager gives a brief talk to a large group of employees and then answers questions—all kinds of questions—for an hour or so. I conduct about a dozen Open Forums a year. The questions I need to deal with at these meetings test my knowledge of the affairs of the company, its divisions, and its plants as well as my integrity and managerial mettle. In many ways they remind me of the examination I had to pass before I was granted my Ph.D.—the infamous "qualifying exam." The large group of assembled employees collectively possess immense knowledge and a wide variety of interests. Facing their questions serves to hone my managerial capabilities as well as to keep me reasonably humble.

Today I manage a company that in 1985 was ranked by *Fortune* magazine as the 226th largest in the United States. *Dun's*, another business magazine, a few years ago described us as one of the five best-managed companies in the country, and *Electronic Business* magazine, in 1986, named us the best company in our field. In a recent book we were listed among *The 100 Best Companies to Work For in America*. We compete with the "Big Boys" of international industry, and I think we have managed to create a work environment that is hard-charging and at the same time human. I like to think that some of my personal attitudes and convictions—which run through this book—have helped to make it so.

In the following pages I attempt to give you the essence of two decades of experience in managing. I do that by walking you through some particularly pertinent real-life questions and also by sharing some recollections of relevant personal experiences. As you read along, I think you'll agree that managing is highly stimulating work: Realizing that you initiated a change for the better can be a wonderful "high."

You don't have to be the president of a company to feel the excitement that comes from bringing about change. You merely need to work in the company of people—as their boss, their employee, or their peer. That's what managing at work is about.

I Hate My Boss!

I was surprised to find that a large proportion of the letters I received dealt with the writer's difficulties in getting along with his or her boss. But maybe I shouldn't have been surprised. After all, work matters a great deal to most people, more than they usually let on. Who would be their "most significant other" at work if not their boss? He or she is the one who hired them, introduced them to their work, corrects them, criticizes (too much?) and praises (not enough?), gives them their raise (they hope), and smiles or scowls at them.

Bosses, as reflected in the letters I've received, are not a perfect bunch. Again, this should not be surprising. For one thing, the employees of super bosses may not write for advice. For another, the work of managing others is a tricky task, and there can be no apprenticeship for it. So most managers sort of "learn-as-they-go," sometimes by watching their own bosses at work, and often from their own employees.

I still remember sitting in the first business meeting I have ever attended. I sat in the furthest corner, completely overwhelmed by the whole scene, not understanding much of the discussion at all and watching the interchange between my boss, who was conducting the meeting, and the others there. That experience was my first lesson in how to conduct a meeting.

I remember another incident when, as a new supervisor, I found myself extremely uncomfortable with my newly acquired right to tell others, who the week before had been my peers, what to do. I was very tentative, unsure of how to handle things, and went to incredible lengths to persuade and convince my subordinates that the way I wanted to proceed was the right way, in fact, the *only* right way. After a while, one of them pulled me aside and told me that I was wasting everybody's time. He pointed out that the differences between the various approaches just weren't worth making such a big fuss over and urged me just to tell them—plainly *tell* them—what to do.

And, I also remember some time later receiving a fifteen-page hand-written letter from a man who reported to me. He pointed out in extremely personal terms how my critical comments and especially my sarcasm (and I thought I was just being funny!) affected him; how his motivation was dampened whenever I made a joke at his expense. I was stunned to realize how things I said were heard by a subordinate. What to me seemed like minor matters were greatly magnified and amplified by my position.

You don't learn these things in school. You learn by watching, by doing, and by listening to the feedback. You learn from your own mistakes—and, if you are smart, also from the mistakes of others.

A SUPERVISOR CAN DESTROY AN EMPLOYEE'S SELF-IMAGE

QUESTION

I work as a clerk for a small company. My supervisor got into the habit of blaming me for everything that goes wrong. No matter what happens, I am the one that gets singled out, sometimes jokingly, sometimes seriously. It's reached the point where I'm beginning to lose confidence in myself. I've tried to talk to my supervisor about it, but he doesn't take me seriously. What should I do?

ANSWER

Run, don't walk, to the nearest exit—quit! Once you become the habitual butt of jokes, it's all but impossible to change that perception. It sounds like you are in danger of adopting that same image of yourself. Don't! If that happens, you will carry this problem to every new workplace. Get a fresh start in a different environment as soon as possible—the quality of your future work career is at stake.

> Our bosses are important to us because, like our parents, they are sources of approval and disapproval. Like the relationship between parent and child, the relationship between boss and employee is a sensitive one. Should it be a close one or a distant one? Should you make friends with your boss or your employees, or should you keep the relationship limited strictly to work?
>
> I have always followed the principle that I make friends with whomever I want to; if we happen to work together, so much the better. Having friends at work makes work more enjoyable and can even help tide you over difficulties. But this is not how everyone approaches this issue. For some reason, there is an all-too-widely held view that work and social relationships don't mix.

MANAGING AND HAVING FUN ARE NOT MUTUALLY EXCLUSIVE

QUESTION

I work in a small sandwich shop and have worked there for over three years. I am one of the original employees of this restaurant and am in line to become a manager. I have a good time at work and do a lot of socializing with my coworkers. This in no way detracts from the job I do and makes it a lot more fun.

My problem is that I have heard that this would not be acceptable as a manager. In other words, I would have to change the way I act if I become a manager. Is this true? Is it impossible for me to have fun and also manage other people?

ANSWER

There is *nothing* that says you can't have fun if your job is to manage! On the contrary, I believe your effectiveness in motivating and organizing your staff, as well as your ability to communicate with them, will be enhanced if you bring a natural and energetic approach to your work area—along with a bit of humor.

Your sense of enjoyment is likely to infect your coworkers and employees, and you will be seen as more approachable with work problems. All of this in turn will enhance your ability to get results from your group.

However, you do need to learn when to turn serious. You are being paid to provide a service to your customers, and when you run into problems and difficulties you must approach them with a purposeful and no-nonsense manner.

When you run into performance problems with your subordinates, you need to handle them straightforwardly and effectively—notwithstanding that yesterday you may have been socializing with them. In other words, you'll need to learn how and when to switch into the appropriate mode.

This isn't an easy skill to acquire, and some managers may choose not even to try; instead they develop a more distant personal attitude toward their employees so they don't have to learn. In my view, this is a pity. Everybody loses, including the manager, who will find work less enjoyable because of his or her distant attitude.

EIGHT HOURS WITHOUT A SMILE

If you want to see what work can be like without a bit of human touch, just read on.

QUESTION

I'd like to work for a supervisor who cares about me as a person—not just as a subordinate. All my current boss cares about is business. She's so cold and insensitive that the atmosphere in our office is as heavy as lead.

Am I out of order even to worry about such things? I hope you'll understand what it's like to work eight hours a day without one smile.

ANSWER

I do—and I don't think you are out of order at all. Work is too important a part of your life to be spent in an oppressive environment. In addition, I'm convinced that relationships with people on the job are very important elements of our desire to work and perform.

I suggest that you tell your supervisor about your feelings, but I don't think it will do any good; she sounds like a person who is unlikely to change. As long as she's a good supervisor in the work sense, perhaps you can make up for what she cannot supply by developing closer ties with your coworkers. It's important to have such relationships at work, but it isn't absolutely necessary that they be with your boss.

THE "SERF" RESENTS THE DICTATOR

Many bosses are seen by their employees as being, well, too bossy.

QUESTION

I work for a small, owner-managed company. The owner has hired some other managers, but he continues to run the place as his personal fiefdom, interfering with whatever issue catches his fancy, dispensing favors or punishment on a whim.

My own supervisor just lets all this happen. I feel very troubled by this scene but haven't figured out what I should (or can) do to change it. What do you suggest?

ANSWER

I am afraid I can't hold out a great deal of encouragement for you. Owner-run companies are often run in an arbitrary, dictatorial way. In fact, often that is what limits their growth. Some owners recognize this and gradually modify their behavior, permitting their managers to take over and replace their capricious actions with consistent managerial processes. Others never do; they would rather let their company be strangled than give up their hold on it.

If you feel that your owner will eventually recognize that his behavior might limit his company's growth, stay at the job. Perhaps as the right occasion arises, you can mention the problem to the owner. But be aware that dictators sometimes come down hard on the bearers of bad news. If that risk is too much for you, look for another job. And try to evaluate a new employer carefully, so you don't exchange serfhood in one fiefdom for the same position in another.

A VOLATILE MANAGER RATTLES HIS EMPLOYEES

If I were to take a poll, I think it would show that one of the top complaints about bosses has to do with their tendency to let their tempers fly. Partly, this is probably a matter of perception: What might be dismissed as a little irritability in another sounds more serious and threatening coming from a person in a position of authority. But partly it is real: Some people in authority go unchallenged too long for their own and their organization's good.

QUESTION

My boss has a very bad temper. The other day in a meeting we were exchanging ideas, and he just blew up. I was shocked and thought his reaction was totally inappropriate to the situation. Five minutes later, after he had gotten rid of his anger (at my expense), he was fine. But now I'm hesitant about expressing myself, as well as insecure about my relationship with him.

I don't know how to handle this situation. Can you offer any suggestions?

ANSWER

Your problem illustrates why managers must learn to control their tempers. If they are unpredictable in any way, they foster insecurity in their employees, who then won't, or can't, do their best for the organization.

Catch your boss at a time when he seems to be in a stable mood. Ask to talk to him privately (this is very important: "Audiences" bring out the worst in people with volatile tempers). Tell him frankly that you feel insecure and hesitant out of fear of triggering his temper. If you manage to time the discussion well, you'll probably find that he agrees with you completely. I am afraid, however, that even if the discussion does go well, it won't prevent future outbursts. The most you can expect is a reduction in their frequency. The violent temper is probably part of your boss's personality.

If you feel that aside from your boss's outbursts your work situation is rewarding, be patient and persevere. But gird yourself to going through such occurrences of bad temper and subsequent discussions from time to time. If you are not up to it, consider moving on.

Fortunately, not all pleas for advice are for such serious situations. Many letters are merely reflections of the fact that bosses are ordinary human beings with the same faults as anybody else. Dealing with these requires little more than a bit of tact and patience.

MY SUPERVISOR JUST GOES ON AND ON . . .

QUESTION
Whenever I ask my supervisor a question about a procedure, I get a lecture instead of a yes or no answer. Should I let him finish his dissertation, or should I interrupt him and tell him that a yes or no is all I need?

ANSWER
Cutting your supervisor off strikes me as a rude way of dealing with a harmless bad habit. Instead, try to phrase your question in such a way that a brief answer is elicited. For instance, start by saying, "Can you please tell me quickly," or, "I only have a minute—can you tell me if . . ."

MY MANAGER IS IMPATIENT AND SHE MAKES ME FEEL DUMB

QUESTION
A few months ago our branch office was consolidated with another one in the next town in order to cut costs. It was a hard adjustment for everybody because we had our own way of doing things and they had theirs.

I have been having problems with one of the managers from the other office who explains their procedures so fast that I often miss some points. If I ask her again, she puts me down with a sarcastic comment. I've tried talking to her, but she makes it seem like it's my problem. I'm running out of solutions—and patience. Do you have any suggestions?

ANSWER

The procedures that this manager is trying to explain to you must be second nature to her; therefore, anyone who has trouble catching on seems dense to her. She certainly isn't demonstrating much empathy, but I suggest that you muster up more patience.

Time is your ally in this situation. The new and weird ways of the other office will soon be familiar, and your manager will be amazed at how "smart" you have become!

MY BOSS MAKES ME DO GRUBBY WORK

QUESTION

How can I stop my boss from taking advantage of me? I am a clerk in a department store. I don't know if being a new employee has anything to do with my problem, but my manager is in the habit of asking me to do little tasks that other managers usually do for themselves. For example, one day she had me answer the phone when she was bending down right next to it and I was five feet away. Another time she had me walking back and forth from the phone to where she was, telling her what the person on the phone wanted. She could easily have taken the call herself.

There are other little incidents that may not be a big deal to anyone but me. One or two are all right, but more than that and it becomes hard to swallow. What would you recommend to a new employee with this problem?

ANSWER

I think you are being altogether too sensitive. Stop being so self-indulgent and buckle down to do your work. As a new employee, you should dedicate yourself to being as helpful to your coworkers and your supervisor as you can, and to learning as much about your new job as possible. Don't worry about what tasks are suitable for you, worry about making a contribution!

Well, my response to the last letter didn't earn me much popularity. The return mail brought this blast and others like it.

A READER'S RESPONSE

I was absolutely appalled with your response to the department-store clerk who felt that her boss was taking advantage of her. Your answer sounded like that of an antiquated, chauvinistic manager: "Be nice and everything will be just fine!" In other words, bury your feelings if you think you're being taken advantage of. Just knuckle down and work on making a contribution to the department. (Isn't that what men have been saying to women and minorities all these years?)

The reality of the situation is that the employee will never make a contribution unless he or she is treated like an equal and a contributing individual. In addition, the employee cannot make a contribution if he or she (mostly she) spends time catering to others.

Perhaps a better response to the question would have been for you to encourage the writer to talk to her supervisor in private and verbalize her feelings about the behavior. After all, it is rude to keep a third party waiting on the telephone while you confer with another for the appropriate response. Encouraging "open communication" can do wonders in establishing rapport and improving performance.

Incidentally, there is no such thing as "being too sensitive." People who claim another is "too sensitive" have been around computers too long.

One advantage of being the columnist is that you can have the last word.

ANSWER

Everything can be taken to extremes. Of course, talking to your boss and telling him or her how you feel about things is a good thing. Of course, open communications are key to making a work group function well. But using these to express dissatisfaction with trivial matters is like taking antibiotics to cure a common cold.

Try to keep in mind that the irritating incidents probably have another side. Perhaps the supervisor was busy looking for merchandise for another customer when the phone rang. Perhaps she was trying to have you learn how to handle the calls on your own. Be that as it may, I think it is better to shrug some of these annoyances off and *not* make a big deal out of them—or else we'll be doing nothing but discussing our feelings the whole workday.

2

You Have the Right
to Be Managed

WHAT does it mean to be managed? It means getting the time and attention of a knowledgeable person who is *paid to provide it*—your boss. It means getting trained in the rudiments of the job, getting coached, getting evaluated (praised or criticized—whichever is appropriate). It means getting encouragement when you are bogged down and getting a kick in the butt when you are the victim of spring fever. It means having somebody to talk to, whether it is about a machine that doesn't work right or about your career objectives.

Too bad not enough of this happens.

EVERY EMPLOYEE HAS THE RIGHT TO BE MANAGED

QUESTION

My boss hardly supervises me. She assigns my work by writing on a board labeled "Today's Work." Usually she just writes a simple phrase, and I often run into problems because I don't quite understand what she means. But I can't ask her because she's either in a meeting or locked in her office doing reports. When I run into problems, she gets mad at me, but she still doesn't give me any direction. What should I do?

QUESTION

I am a new manager and I'm having trouble getting the time I need with my boss. He's always too busy to keep his appointments with me. I feel that I'm barely staying on top of things, while with some guidance I could make a real contribution. How can I get the help I need without appearing incapable of doing my job?

ANSWER

Both of you need to invoke what I consider to be the most important right of any employee: *the right to be managed.* This is as basic as the right to a paycheck. If your paycheck was withheld, you would undoubtedly holler bloody murder and pursue the matter until you received satisfaction. You should demand access to your respective bosses with the same conviction and vigor.

All managers recognize their employees' right to be paid, but when it comes to their right to be supervised, things get less clear. Furthermore, the manager who isn't readily available to help you with your daily work probably won't sit still for a lecture on this subject. So, look for a way to communicate your need to your supervisors without putting them on the defensive. For instance, you could put your thoughts in a confidential letter. Explain your difficulties just as you did in your questions, but flesh out your case with examples where you could have done a better job for them and for your company if you had more guidance along the way.

What all this ultimately boils down to is that you need more time with your boss. *Ask for it!* Indicate your flexibility; offer to meet early in the day or late, whichever way is easier on him or her, but persist, gently but steadfastly, in your request. The reasonableness of what you are asking will eventually prevail.

As I read these questions and others like them, I couldn't help concluding that while these employees have valid complaints, they've done little or nothing about them. It's almost as if in the employees' minds managers are supposed to know what to do, and if they don't do it, there must be some weighty reason. Unfortunately, that's frequently not the case, and managers, just like all other workers, must often be reminded of their responsibilities.

It's not possible to improve the manager-employee working relationship without both parties investing *time* in it. And so I usually end up encouraging the employee to press for undisturbed *one-on-one* time with his or her manager. Such time can then be used to fix whatever is lacking in their collaboration. And there can be quite a variety of elements that need fixing.

HOW TO GET YOUR BOSS TO ADD VALUE TO YOUR WORK

QUESTION

I'm an insurance salesman and I happen to like the profession. My problem is that my boss is an ex–insurance salesman turned manager. While he used to be a star salesman, he doesn't know the first thing about being a manager.

I want and need someone to manage me. I don't think I'm nearly as successful as I could be if I had a leader, a role model, someone with whom I could kick my ideas around (all the things I thought managers should do).

I've asked him for help, and it isn't that he doesn't want to give it, he doesn't know how. I just continue to do my job as I always have, and he just continues to push paper. Can I get to where I need to be without a manager?

ANSWER

You say your boss once was a good salesman. Since you are a salesman yourself, there must be a lot of things you could learn from him. Take the initiative and try to mine his experience and knowledge.

Make sure you can spend uninterrupted time with him. Arrange to meet *regularly* in his office. If no other time is available, do it at breakfast or at lunch. Try various approaches until you find a setup that is convenient and works for both of you.

As you establish this pattern, use it to get help for your real day-to-day problems. Experiment in various ways: Bring him specific questions dealing with your sales situations and ask him how he would have handled them. Ask him to make some sales calls with you and then critique you; and from time to time encourage him to take over the handling of a particular situation, just so you'll have an opportunity to watch *him* in action.

In other words, create situations where you can learn from your boss's experience as a salesman. I believe that once he realizes that he has been able to help you, he'll pick up the ball and run with it.

NO TIME FOR TRAINING, ONLY FOR CRITICISM

QUESTION

For several months I was employed at a store and had a lot of trouble with my boss, the owner. He never had time to train me because he was always "swamped." Instead, whenever I made an error he yelled at me in front of customers. My coworkers were put in the position of having to apologize for his conduct. The turnover at the store was incredible.

After a few months I'd had enough. I found another job and quit. My boss acted as if I had stabbed him in the back; he told me he was planning to train me just as I was leaving. How should I handle such a situation if I ever encounter it again?

ANSWER

Simply don't put up with it. It sounds like you accepted demeaning and unproductive treatment from your boss for too long before you decided to quit. That's wrong. If it happens to you again, don't save up your frustration over the situation: Act on it.

After you realize that your boss's behavior follows a predictably bad pattern, confront him and state your feelings in a straightforward way. Also, use this discussion to ask for further training.

And remember, you get paid to perform a service, not to take personal abuse.

WHERE DOES STYLE END AND PERFORMANCE BEGIN?

QUESTION

My problem involves figuring out what to do to please my boss. Several of my peers are extroverts, and they form an "inner circle," a kind of advisory panel. I am part of a less vocal group whose contribution is simply to produce. Personally, I feel our contributions should also be recognized and rewarded. With my manager, however, if special kudos are forthcoming, it's usually only the "inner circle" that gets them.

Should he try to elicit greater participation and interaction among us, the less vocal group, or should we try to emulate the extroverts in order to please him?

ANSWER

Discuss your observations with your boss. If you feel that he favors a particular style, tell him so. I think it's important that the two of you agree on where style ends and performance begins. Listen to him. He may, for instance, argue that the coworkers whom you describe as extroverts have an easier time responding to changing situations in a quick and timely fashion. If that's the case, even if their intelligence and efforts are otherwise similar to yours, their contributions may in fact be more valuable.

While I don't think you should try to change your personality, you may learn about things that you can do to enhance your contributions so that you too can earn more kudos along the way.

Once somebody asked me to identify the single most useful management technique that I learned through my years of managing. My answer was: the practice of regularly scheduled *one-on-one* meetings.

I can't overstate the usefulness of such sessions. They serve as a *universal medium* through which the endless variety of problems that develop between boss and employee can be identified, worked on, improved, and fixed. One-on-one meetings provide an opportunity for the manager to teach and coach his employees. At the same time, they permit him or her to learn from the employee about his problems, observations, the guts of his work, and his reaction to what the boss does and does not do. Such one-on-one sessions encourage employees to open up with their boss, something that otherwise they might not do.

Stating it another way, I don't know how anyone can manage without them!

The key to making such meetings truly effective is to have them *regularly* (schedule them once a week or once every two weeks for at least one hour so you have time to deal with complex and sensitive issues), and to make the employee feel that he *owns* the meeting and can bring up whatever subject he is preoccupied with. This point is critical—it's the only way the employee can direct the discussion in ways that will help him with his day-to-day problems and bring up touchy subjects like the boss's attitude toward training or the style of the "inner circle." Stopping in the hallway for an impromptu chat is *not* a substitute for a one-on-one meeting—can you imagine such subjects being dealt with on the fly?

For you managers who are throwing up your hands, exclaiming that you don't have time for such luxuries, let me stress that one-on-one meetings will *save you time* (honestly!) by eliminating many of the irregular *ad hoc* exchanges you are involved in today.

    I remember sitting in a plant manager's office watching his employees stick their heads in to ask a quick question, only to be interrupted by the phone ringing with another employee on the line with an inquiry. I *knew* beyond a shadow of a doubt that most of these interruptions could be avoided if the manager adopted the practice of regular one-on-one meetings. But could I convince the frazzled manager of this? No way—he just shook his head with that "you-just-don't-understand" look as he reached to pick up the phone again.

    A year or so later, the man sheepishly approached me with calendar in hand. By now he was so overwhelmed by the demands on his time, he was ready to try anything. We discussed his schedule and habits, and he returned to his office, determined to try to channel his dealings into regular, predictable meetings. I can see the same skeptical look on your face, dear reader, as you read this; but the fact is, it worked! The man got his head above water and has kept it there ever since.

    One-on-one meetings are the *preventive medicine* of management work—even if they are resisted by the patient in the same way.

3

The Boss Must Bring Something to the Party

A manager must *add value* to the work of his or her employees. Too many managers view themselves as passive conduits of communication between higher and lower echelons in the organization, bringing information or instructions from one level to the next. This is wrong. *A manager must bring something to the party.* The work and work habits of employees should be enhanced through the manager's work. He should cause his workers to become more productive, more efficient, and capable of generating progressively higher-quality work.

He or she can do this in a variety of ways. For instance, he can share his superior technical knowledge or his experience (he can *teach* his employees how to do their jobs better); and he can make sure that others in the organization know about an employee's work and that the employee knows about developments elsewhere that might affect his work. The manager can add value by eliminating duplication of work and by starting projects to improve things. He can add value by saving an employee from a dangerous stumble or by leaving him to his own devices when he is ready to spread his wings. He can add value by setting clear objectives and by being a good role model for others around him. Most importantly, he can create a work environment in which all employees will *want* to make a contribution.

MAKING CHOICES IS A KEY PART OF THE JOB

The specific course of action a manager takes will often be controversial. In time, it will be obvious if he was right or wrong, but at the time of the decision, it always looks like he is choosing between close alternatives, like choosing which way to go at a fork in the road. The distance between the two branches at first is very small, even though the roads will eventually diverge greatly. Being right at these close calls is perhaps the ultimate value a manager brings to the workplace.

QUESTION

My father works for a computer company. While working on a project, he requested a design change that would have saved tens of thousands of dollars over the life of the product. His request was denied on the grounds that making the change would have increased the department's costs in that quarter. Shouldn't management be thinking of the future that lies beyond the quarterly statements?

ANSWER

Yes, management must think beyond the quarterly statement, but that doesn't necessarily mean that they should have made this particular design change. Suppose, for example, that this company had a thousand dollars a month to spend. If they spend more than what they have coming in, they will eventually go out of business and your father would find himself without a job.

Now, what is the best way to spend the thousand dollars? The design improvement your father was advocating was one thing it could have been spent on. As you say in your letter, it could have saved tens of thousands of dollars in the years to come. But there were probably other choices. Perhaps there was a new product someone was proposing that could propel the company way ahead of its competition. Such a product could generate a lot of additional profits that might even make it possible, at a later stage, to implement the improvements advocated by your father.

Of course, neither I nor you know the real situation at this company. It's impossible for us to tell without knowing their reasoning whether or not the managers were unduly influenced by the current quarter—but they are not automatically wrong. The point is, management always has to make *choices,* for instance, between one investment and another.

So long as they add value . . .

MANAGERS WILL BE AROUND FOR A WHILE

QUESTION

There are millions of personal computers in offices today, with many more being bought every day. Will these computers eventually eliminate the need for middle managers?

ANSWER

I don't believe that they ever will. Computers can automate the mechanics of work of all kinds—whether they generate payroll checks or perform sophisticated statistical analyses. So far, they cannot even come close to doing the kind of work that involves *judgment* on the part of managers.

When a manager hires or promotes a person, he or she relies on a collection of very wide-ranging observations, digested, sorted, and weighted against a set of complex criteria. When he or she perceives the need for a new product or service and sees an unfulfilled commercial opportunity behind what today is just a set of problems, he draws on intuition honed by experience. Such processes aren't easily reduced to a set of computer programs—not today or in the foreseeable future.

But even if computers eventually become "smart" enough to do these types of chores, they still won't be able to substitute for managers in their role as catalysts for the communication that *must* take place among employees at the workplace. Even flesh-and-blood managers have a hard time coping with the complex needs, aspirations, insecurities, and conflicts of their coworkers. On this account alone, I think that the jobs of human managers will be around indefinitely.

One of the simplest ways a manager can add value is by removing bottlenecks and obstacles from the way of his employees. When I was a young engineer, I got embroiled in a scientific dispute with a co-worker. It wasn't a huge thing; we didn't agree on the interpretation of some experimental results. Each of us was totally certain about his own point of view; neither could persuade the other. After a while, the scientific disagreement became a heated personal feud, preoccupying both of us and rendering us quite ineffective in our daily work.

Eventually our boss got into the act. He shuffled some work assignments so that the two of us had little to do with each other. Our previously all-abiding interest in the contested issue quickly cooled, and we became our normal, productive selves again. Our boss clearly added value to the work of his department by eliminating a roadblock (even if it was one of our own making!)

It was a simple, obvious thing to do. Or was it? After all, the point in dispute was *not* resolved, just set aside. Our manager had to make two decisions: one, in a matter of *substance* (is this issue critical enough that it needs to be resolved, even at the cost of losing Andy's and Joe's efficiency—or can it be left alone without hurting the overall project?); and two, in a matter of *timing* (have Andy and Joe had enough time to resolve this issue on their own? Will they sort it out if they are given another few days?).

To answer these questions properly, our manager had to be quite knowledgeable in the work performed in our group. This is always necessary. I simply can't subscribe to the notion that "a manager can manage anything." Far from it. To be in a position to add value, the manager must at least be familiar with the guts of the work performed by his or her people, even though he clearly cannot be an expert in all aspects of their work.

KNOW THY CHOSEN FIELD

This issue—what a manager needs to know—is often on people's minds. Students are particularly concerned with it.

QUESTION

I am a business student interested in eventually becoming an executive, preferably in a high-technology company. How should I prepare myself for such a career?

ANSWER

The best way anyone can prepare for a management career is by mastering a particular field.

For instance, it is the best salesman who should be promoted to sales manager or the best accountant who should be made accounting manager. Therefore, if you want to move up in a company, become proficient in a field by concentrating your studies in it. It could be accounting, production planning, or human-resource management—whatever it is, become good at it.

Competence in your chosen field should earn you the desired promotions and will also help after you start managing others. Your employees will respect your expertise, and their respect will make your task of leading them that much easier.

And from another student:

QUESTION

Must a manager be able to perform all the jobs in his department?

ANSWER

In an ideal world, a manager *would* be able to perform all the jobs in his department. In reality, this is rarely possible. The manager hopefully came up through the ranks and is familiar with *some* of the jobs in the department. A good boss will also strive to learn from the people under his supervision as much as possible. He'll work to learn about their jobs. Such knowledge enables the manager to help his employees and will also aid him in coordinating the different types of work performed by his group.

4

Managers Come in All Shapes and Styles

QUESTION

I am an engineering student. Eventually, I would like to become a manager. I'd like to know, what are the characteristics of individuals who become successful managers?

How many times have I been asked this question? I can't begin to count. Somehow people have the idea that if they just *act* a certain way, they'll become good managers or good leaders.

In fact, there isn't a single set of individual characteristics that one can associate with effective managers. Through the years, I have worked with individuals who were:

- extroverted and introverted
- dynamic and cautious
- patient and impatient
- colorful and boring

and I've seen all types both *make* the grade and *not* make it.

The important point is, effective managers are distinguished by what they accomplish, not by what they are. Different individuals can make things happen by different methods, relying on their own personal capabilities. A person who is patient and thorough, for instance, can use those strengths to achieve the desired results, while another who is imaginative and has a good intuitive grasp of situations can make those attributes work for him.

Two examples come to mind. One is a very successful manager who could have made a cartoon character: hopelessly disorganized in thought as well as in how he did things, jumping from one item to another with great energy, frequently leaving unfinished tasks in his wake. Yet he had a phenomenal intuition on what was the next truly important thing in his business. It was as if he could see around corners. His constantly working mind, which created the impression of disorganization, was always probing possibilities and probabilities. When he latched onto something, he could devote his whole being to the task of enlisting everybody around him to support him in his pursuit, almost always successfully.

This man then combined his key strengths, the ability to spot trends before they became clear to others and his ability to persuade his colleagues to help make up for his major weaknesses: lack of organization and consistency. As it turns out, the combination was a very effective one.

Another individual I know is the total opposite. Quiet, self-effacing, prone to sitting through meetings hardly asking any questions or offering comments, consistent and organized to the point of being boring, and persistent, persistent, persistent. I have known this man for some twenty years, seen him work on a wide variety of problems, and have yet to see him fail. He uses his strengths, which are quite the opposite of those of the first individual, to achieve results of similar magnitude and quality. If you saw these two people side by side, you would have a hard time believing that they *both* could be successful.

So, I advise aspiring managers to stop worrying about what magic characteristics they need; instead I urge them to concentrate on the task at hand and use their own strengths and capabilities to the best effect. One should constantly be on the lookout to identify what works, continue to do it, figure out what doesn't, and stop.

People are not very satisfied with this answer. They continue to badger me: "Don't you think an effective manager has to be . . ." and here you can add words like personable, strong-willed, charismatic, decisive, or what have you. It's almost as if people had romantic ideas of what managers should look and act like from watching grade-B movies.

The truth is a lot simpler—and at the same time, infinitely more complicated. *A manager is effective if he produces results.* Period.

I never quite get away with this answer in face-to-face conversations, so I will relent and provide a few observations that, in my view, are applicable to most managerial situations.

GIVE-AND-TAKE IS ESSENTIAL

QUESTION

Is it better for a manager to be informal and involved, or more distant and impersonal?

QUESTION

I work for a relatively small eight-year-old manufacturing company. The president of the company, who has been there since the beginning, remains very involved with our daily work; he interacts constantly with lower-level employees and hands out his share of "discipline." Should a man in his position continue to deal with lower-level employees, or should he delegate this task to his managers?

QUESTION

I have been on my job for two months, and my first review is due soon. My boss spends most of his time in meetings. He rarely comes by to check up on my work and makes no effort to talk to me. How can he make a fair and accurate judgment of my performance?

ANSWER

Managing is often defined as getting things done through people. A manager's work, therefore, *must* involve interaction and give-and-take with other people, especially his employees. That's the best way for managers to learn what they are doing, and that's also the best way to communicate what they should be doing. So, my answer to the *first reader* is that a manager who is involved with the work of his employees is likelier to do a better job than one who is distant.

More power to the president of the *second reader*'s company for being involved with the work of lower-level employees. I hope he can continue to do so even as the company grows. But in order to permit the managers under him to do *their* work, he should follow a basic rule: While it is perfectly OK for him to deal directly with their employees (ask questions, offer advice), he should be careful to give *directions* only through the managers who supervise these employees directly. Otherwise, he will undermine these managers and render them ineffective.

The *third reader*'s comments illustrate what happens when a manager stays distant from his employees. Clearly, he will have a very difficult time evaluating their work—a key role of all managers. All I can suggest in this case is that *you* should prepare for your review. Document, in writing, *your own view* of your accomplishments. Keep it factual, stay with measurable items—do not offer a subjective evaluation. Hand these comments to your boss at review time, suggesting that they might aid him in evaluating your work. But, unfortunately, nothing will substitute for an involved, observant supervisor.

DON'T INTIMIDATE YOUR SUBORDINATES

QUESTION

I have a manager who intimidates me. He is often nice and friendly, but every once in a while he just blows up at me. At such times he says things that hurt my feelings and make me want to shrivel up inside. I find myself anxious to please him and do what he wants just so he goes away.

Do managers make people on the bottom feel this way on purpose? How can we cope with such approaches?

ANSWER

Such behavior is terrible! Managers should go out of their way to *avoid* intimidating their employees. Not only is intimidation an unsavory practice, it is also bad for the workings of the organization. Intimidated workers won't put their hearts and minds into doing their jobs well; they will suppress ideas for fear of calling attention to themselves, and this can only hurt the business.

Now, you should understand that managers are human. They have weak points, bad days, and insecurities of their own. Sometimes they may feel threatened by circumstances at the workplace or by a particular employee. They may lash out or otherwise act in a way that intimidates their employees just so they can gain some time and regain their balance. It's not right, but it will happen.

Learn to handle such events by looking at them as if they were a storm: big gusts of wind that will blow over after a while. Don't fight the gusts while they are blowing, but resume dealing with your boss in a normal fashion once they pass.

Keep in mind that while intimidating your employees is *always* bad, there are times when it is necessary and appropriate for a manager to take a firm, unequivocal position on issues. For example, when employees have little or no experience with the job at hand, the right thing to do is to tell them *what* to do, *how* to do it, *when* to do it— without resorting to much (or any) consultation. This management style can be described as autocratic (a bad-sounding word), yet it is the correct approach under such circumstances.

On the other hand, if the employees are experienced in their work, their boss should just make sure that they understand the objectives of the task. Detailed instructions are neither necessary nor appropriate. Judging what style of management is appropriate in a given situation is one of the marks of an effective manager.

TOUGHNESS IS A STATE OF MIND

This all leads to a question that is pretty close to home. In 1984, in a survey, *Fortune* magazine listed me as one of the "ten toughest managers" in the U.S. As you may imagine, subsequently I got quite a few questions on how I interpreted this dubious honor.

In my view, toughness is a state of mind, not a style of behavior. Toughness in management does not mean banging on the table, being mean and intimidating to your workers, or being insensitive to their needs. Instead, it reflects a dedication to achieving success for the enterprise and, through it, for its customers, employees, and stockholders.

A tough-minded manager is one who can reason his way to the correct course of action without being seduced by what is easy.

A tough manager is like a good coach. He drives his team toward outstanding performance, demands a lot from his players, spurs them on, praises and criticizes them freely to reach a common goal.

It is a lot harder to be tough than to be mean—but it's also more effective.

Here is an example.

QUESTION

I am an office manager at a junior college. I supervise about five people. Lately, I have been having problems with one of them. She is an older woman, a single mother of six. Her children's ages range from eighteen to thirty-six, and four of them are students at our school.

This employee is going through a divorce and she conducts a lot of her legal work over the phone during her work hours. During a typical working day, our office also gets ten to fifteen personal calls for her. To compound all this, the children who attend the college come into the office numerous times each day.

The combination of the divorce and the children clearly interferes with this person's work. We are in a busy period and really cannot afford to lose her contribution. What should I do?

ANSWER

You have no choice but to confront your employee with the problem her conduct is causing. In fact, you should have done so already; in my view, you have permitted the development of an untenable situation.

Adopt a step-by-step approach. First, take your employee aside and describe the problem just as you have done in your letter. Be gentle in your approach, but don't be apologetic: You have a job to do, you need her contribution, and you are not getting it. Your employee is the one who needs to be apologetic, not you. Ask her to arrange her personal affairs so that their impact on her work is minimized. For instance, if she needs to attend to her divorce during working hours, she should make up the time lost after hours. In addition, she ought to eliminate all other distractions.

While your employee will probably agree to do what you ask, there is a good chance that her behavior won't change in a lasting manner. Be prepared to follow up your first discussion with a more determined confrontation. Remind the employee of your previous discussion and make more specific demands this time. Insist that the distracting behavior stop; set specific limits as to how much of it you will find tolerable. Arrange at this time for another meeting where you would evaluate her follow-through.

If your employee's performance doesn't improve, start formal disciplinary steps.

YOU CAN ONLY LEARN TO MANAGE BY DOING IT

Unlike many other professions, there is really no formal training that prepares a person to be a manager. Business schools give a student theoretical tools, even descriptions of managerial situations through the case-study method, but don't—and can't—give the aspiring manager a chance to practice "getting things done through others." In the workplace, a worker who performs well is often named a manager, and if all goes well, he or she will be sent to take some courses in the subject—no apprenticeship here, either.

In fact, however, a person has more relevant experience than he realizes. Going through life, one spends quite a bit of time organizing and participating in group activities (games, beach parties, family affairs). While the activities involved may be very different from work, the skills one gains are similar.

I made a point earlier in this chapter that a manager must learn what works for him or her and tailor an effective style around those elements. This can only be done by experimenting, by trying and failing, trying again and eventually succeeding.

But how does one experiment at being a manager without being one? From time to time, you'll find that circumstances bring you an opportunity to practice managing. Grab it! Use such opportunities as very valuable practice sessions to determine which of your skills, capabilities, and approaches bring results.

MANAGING WITHOUT FORMAL AUTHORITY: THE BEST WAY TO LEARN

QUESTION

I've been given all of the duties of a supervisor although I can't be formally promoted to the position because of personal constraints. But many of my coworkers don't listen to me when I ask them to do something. I find this very frustrating. What should I do?

QUESTION

I have been named "acting supervisor" and put in charge of seven or eight employees for periods of two weeks. I notice that whenever I'm in charge, work output slows down and tardiness increases. How can I increase my authority and avoid such problems?

ANSWER

Both of you are in positions that provide the most difficult test of supervisory abilities: supervising others without formal, well-defined authority. This is *excellent experience.* Sometimes even managers who are *formally* in charge of a group need to influence the work of individuals who are not under their direct control. So what you learn in coping with your current situations will help you in later managerial assignments.

I assume that you were chosen for your supervisory tasks because you know the work better than others who work there. If so, this should be the basis of your approach: Use your superior knowledge to *convince* your coworkers that what you are asking them to do is the right thing. Be a good role model. Don't try to *act* the role of the boss; work alongside your coworkers and do better than any of them.

If all of this doesn't work, ask your own boss to talk to your employees about these problems *with you around,* so everybody hears the same words. But I would ask for help only as a last resort; if you work it out on your own, you will have learned an extremely valuable skill.

Such situations—supervision without formal authority—are useful in developing management skills. They also serve to grease the machinery of the workplace. Informal management makes the myriad of things that need to take place happen. It also generates controversy.

BUSYBODY OR BOSS? IT'S A DELICATE ISSUE

QUESTION

I work as an administrator in a large company and report directly to the director of the organization. I have a lot of responsibilities, including acting as a supervisor for several other secretaries who are a bit older than I.

My problem is that the secretaries whom I supervise socialize too much during business hours. While I am convinced that this is wrong, I don't know how to handle this situation without appearing as a "know-it-all." Also, I feel I need to stay on good terms with these secretaries.

On the other hand, if I keep letting the situation slide, I may get into trouble when my boss notices this waste of company time. What should I do?

QUESTION

I am a secretary and I have a problem with our vice president's secretary. She has been timing my breaks and has reported to my direct supervisor when I take five minutes more than usual.

How can I delicately tell this woman to mind her own business?

ANSWER

No, these two letters did not come from the same company—
but they sound like they could have. They certainly illustrate both
sides of a fairly common problem.

In many organizations, the senior secretary *acts* as an office
manager and is responsible for work standards and performance
throughout the entire office. This is so even though the secretaries are assigned to individual managers.

Often the responsibilities and authority of this senior person
are not spelled out anywhere—she (or he) has them through
tradition and custom. Yet as these questions indicate, the issues
they have to deal with can be sensitive ones.

Whether the responsibilities of such a senior person have been
clearly defined or not, she is in fact a supervisor. Both she and her
de facto employees must realize this and act accordingly. When
the senior person recognizes a problem—such as the junior secretaries spending too much time socializing—it is part of her job to
address it.

Any manager, no matter what his or her age might be, would
find this a touchy subject—yet it needs to be dealt with. Take the
junior secretaries aside, one at a time, privately; be polite, unemotional, and objective, and tackle the issue, perhaps with an
introduction like, "I am sorry to have to bring this up, but I feel
that you have been spending too much of your time with nonwork
activities . . ."

Throughout the discussion ask for the others' acceptance of the
need to concentrate more on work. I doubt that they'll be overjoyed with having to face such an issue, but steel yourself: Dealing with it comes with the supervisory territory.

Correspondingly, I am afraid I have little sympathy for our
second writer. The vice president's secretary, however clumsily,
is doing her job. Instead of grousing about it, how about heeding
what she is trying to tell you?

This response rankled some.

A READER'S COMMENTS

I could not disagree with you more!

Clearly, the bossy secretary here is determined to take over and show the real supervisor how to run the office. It is a shame that this writer does not have the strength of character to tell Miss Busybody to mind her own business.

The secretary who wrote to you asked for help, and you responded with an answer that is based on supposition. You don't *know* that the busybody here is performing unwritten duties. In fact, I wonder if you would take this position if the principals involved were men rather than mere female secretaries. Isn't it just that women are accustomed to being pushed around?

ANSWER

You are right in one thing: I don't *know* the exact situation in this—or any other—case. I have to rely on my sense of what may be going on and base my answer on it. My sense in this case told me that the senior secretary was absolutely correct in gently attempting to coax the more junior one to concentrate on her work.

I would have answered this question the same way if the principals involved were men. Furthermore, I have always abhorred the phrase "mere secretary" as well as the attitude it represents. Setting high expectations implies respect for an individual. The person here who seems not to value the contributions of the secretary is the boss who permits her to waste her time.

5

Show Is Better Than Tell

A manager is very visible. People are always watching him, consciously and unconsciously. His conduct and his approach *set values* for an entire organization. His actions, in matters large or small, are far more effective in communicating such values than any memo or policy manual.

I first learned this fact through some experiences involving trivial things. At one time, it struck me that practically all the young manufacturing managers at the company I worked for smoked cigars—as did the head of manufacturing. A few years later, when I was a manager myself, I started to wear open shirts and no tie. This style slowly spread throughout my organization.

These are unimportant manifestations of the large shadow we managers can cast; but our style and conduct also tend to set the pattern in far more important areas.

Perhaps in no area is the influence of a manager exerted more by his or her example than in setting the standards for straightforwardness or for political behavior. Time and time again I have found that if the senior person in charge of an organization is a straight shooter, the organization under him will have the same characteristic. On the other hand, if the top person is a political animal, with a tendency toward manipulating people, setting one against the other, telling each a different story, then after a while the organization will inevitably have the same operating style.

When such a political manager is replaced by a straight-shooting type, the latter has a major task on his hands: to recast the way the organization is expected to operate. He cannot do this by issuing a memo that says, "From now on, devious and manipulative behavior won't be sanctioned around here." He can only do it by providing the example for straight dealing himself, consistently, day in and day out. Gradually, the people under him will get the message and will either change their behavior to match the leader's style or depart.

CUSTOMS—GOOD OR BAD—EMANATE FROM THE BOSS

QUESTION

The use of coarse and abusive language seems to be a pervasive practice where I work. I'm particularly troubled that we are exposed to such language from our managers. What can we do to change such a practice?

ANSWER

In my experience, the use of foul language is usually a matter of local (company or department) custom. Unfortunately, such customs are hard to change. If people at the company where you work have been using foul language for a long time, merely complaining to individual offenders won't accomplish much. You need to influence whoever is the major role model to accomplish change.

In a small company, that role model is likely to be the head of the company; in a large one, the division or department head. If you want to make lasting change, you must reach these individuals. Most of them probably don't even realize that they use language that is objectionable to others. A quiet conversation or even a well-reasoned letter will at least change that. Be sure to give these people a strong indication of how much their practice is emulated throughout the organization and how objectionable it has become.

If you manage to communicate the depth of your concern, your leader may try to change his own behavior and consequently that of others around him. Because he is the role model for his environment, he—and only he—is capable of doing that. But habits like this are slow to die, so be patient and be prepared to nudge the role model from time to time.

MANAGER AS PARENT, OR THE OTHER WAY AROUND?

Put in another way, a manager has a parentlike influence over his organization. Like a parent, he or she is a source of approval and disapproval, of discipline and rewards. As with parents, we often aim to be like our manager—hence his or her actions tend to influence us in many subtle ways. It turns out that in some instances the reverse may also be the case: a parent acting at home like a manager!

QUESTION

I am one of ten children. My father is a manager. It seems to me that he often uses the same type of methods to run his family as he does to run his office: He meets with several of us, assigns us tasks, and requires us to report to him when they are complete, evaluates us, and such. Does this make any sense to you?

ANSWER

Yes, it does. In fact, I can see many parallels. Your father deals with other human beings both at work and at home. The basic rules are similar: His dealings should be based on common sense and empathy. He needs to listen to his employees just as he needs to listen to his children. He must communicate with them, guide them, and impart to them the need to achieve goals that are important both to their personal development and to the smooth operation of the company (or family).

He also needs to be a role model. A manager's success is reflected in the success of the group he directs, and a father's success is reflected in how well his family functions and develops.

In fact, I think there are so many similarities between the two roles that managers could probably profit from employing some of the techniques that work for them in their roles as parents, and vice versa. It's an intriguing thought!

GOOD MANAGERS AREN'T INFALLIBLE—AND ADMIT IT

Earlier I commented that it seems sometimes that people get their ideas of what managers are like and how they act from second-rate movies. In these movies, the managers always know what they are doing (unless they are bad-guy managers, in which case they *never* do). The stereotypical manager is always sure and always right. The real-life manager is rarely sure (after all, he deals with close choices most of the time) and is frequently wrong.

QUESTION

I am a student. As a future business graduate, I would like to know if a manager should ever admit a mistake to his employees?

ANSWER

A manager should most certainly admit his mistakes to his employees—or anyone else for that matter. Being a manager is an occupation, just like being a teacher, an auto mechanic, or a dentist; it does not require infallibility.

More importantly, when you are a manager, you will become a role model to your employees, for better or worse. If you don't admit your mistakes, you will communicate to the people under your supervision that they should not admit theirs. If they follow your example, no one will admit to any errors, and therefore no one will learn from them either.

I got a follow-on letter after this.

OWNING UP TO MISTAKES IS A SIGN OF STRENGTH

QUESTION

I agree with one of your recent columns in which you said that managers should admit their mistakes. But I'm a younger woman managing a department that consists mostly of men older than myself. I worry that by admitting my mistakes, I will undermine my hard-won authority. How do I gracefully acknowledge my errors without losing the respect of the men who work for me?

ANSWER

All of us in management (and in teaching, government, even parenting)—men and women, young or old—worry about losing hard-won respect by admitting our mistakes. Yet, in reality, admitting mistakes is a sign of strength, maturity, and fairness.

If you have trouble accepting this, think of what would happen if you did not admit your mistakes. How long would it take before the men in your department recognized what you were doing? What do you think such recognition would do to their respect for you?

The next time you face a situation like this and you feel the urge to make excuses for yourself, *stop*. Seek some privacy and think through what happened and why. Remind yourself that nobody is expected to be perfect. Ask yourself how you would like your employees to handle such a situation. Bear in mind that by owning up to your mistakes, you set an example for them.

BEWARE OF HYPOCRISY IN THE BOSS!

The worst situation is when the boss says one thing and does another. The employee then has to decide whether to follow the explicitly stated rules of the workplace or to emulate the boss—with the two choices contradictory! This poses a real no-win situation and puts the worst kind of stress on the employee, one from which he or she should escape as soon as possible.

QUESTION

I am an office manager and I supervise about ten people. My boss, the general manager, is very strict; she stresses promptness, limits phone conversations, keeps lunches to exactly one hour, to give just a few examples.

While I agree with all this, there is one problem: She *does* exactly the opposite. Because of this, I find it very difficult to tell my employees to follow the rules. I don't know what to do. Should I confront her with this problem? Is it my place to say anything?

QUESTION

I work for a large retail firm. Recently I applied for vacation time but I was turned down because store policy says we cannot take vacations during certain busy periods.

I was upset over this, but I accepted it. Then I discovered that our store manager took off exactly that week. Is this good management action? Do I have to accept it or is there something I can do?

ANSWER

Both of these situations represent terrible managerial practice. A manager's own conduct is the most important way in which the desired practices of an organization are communicated. A manager's promptness makes a statement that promptness is important. When a manager works during a busy period even though it is inconvenient, that communicates an important set of values about customer service. When a manager requires his or her group to do one thing while doing another himself, he communicates a disregard for the stated values of the organization (promptness, customer service). It says that rank is key. It is hypocritical.

Having said that, I don't know what to suggest to either writer! Ordinarily, I would urge you to confront your supervisors and point out the inconsistency between their conduct and the policies they espouse. You should urge them to become proper role models for the organizations they manage.

But I hesitate to do so in these cases simply because managers who act like these two may be inclined to use their supervisory powers to retaliate against criticism. So, taking action has inherent dangers, and only you can decide whether you are ready to face them.

I do feel, however, that if you aren't ready to take the risks associated with confronting your supervisors, you should look for a job elsewhere—the sooner the better. Staying in the environments created by such supervisors will eventually dull your sense of right and wrong, and you'll become like they are. Don't let that happen under any circumstances! Confront or leave—but don't accept.

6

How the Boss Wins

A manager's output *is* the output of his or her organization. A simple statement, yet it's not intuitively obvious to most managers. Why should it be? Most of us have gotten to be managers by distinguishing ourselves at some task—selling, designing, filling out tax returns, whatever. Throughout the years that we were plying our trade, our output was the result of what we personally were doing. Then, one day, we became managers. We were put in charge of others' work. We were now expected to help these others get results, generate output.

This is a huge change! It requires rethinking our goals, changing our self-image from ace doer to coach, roadblock remover, and key assistant to the remaining doers. It takes most of us quite a while to adapt to this new role, and the process is not without frustrations.

I recall how, as a newly named supervisor of other scientists, I sat in a meeting room and listened to a former colleague, now a subordinate, report on work we had done together. He had the task of convincing the audience of the validity of our findings. He had their full attention. As he was answering all their questions, I sat there feeling sorry for myself at being left out of the action. Knowing that later I would have to attend to some messy personnel problems didn't improve my mood either. It all seemed very unfair. I was beginning to grasp the changed nature of my work; my metamorphosis into a manager had begun.

What particularly confounds most new managers is the huge variety of *people issues* that take up so much of their time and attention. They complain that they can't do any "real work" because so much of their time is spent sorting out personnel problems, reconciling disagreements, orchestrating the workers and their work. In time they will come to realize that this is what *managing* is all about.

HANDLING STAFF CONFLICT
IS PART OF THE JOB

QUESTION

I am a senior-level manager, with a staff of ten. My problem involves two employees who are constantly bickering. I often see them arguing out in the corridor, and my weekly staff meetings usually run at least a half hour overtime because of their battles.

Their areas of responsibility overlap at times, so their contact can't be minimized. But their combat is becoming disruptive to the business. Should I interfere or just let them fight it out?

ANSWER

Handling this conflict is not interference, it's part of your job! As a manager, you are responsible for the output and productivity of the team made up of your employees. Any energy your team members expend fighting each other takes away from their ability to do their job. Take aggressive action to stop the bickering.

Start by sitting down with each of them separately. Tell them that the in-fighting is impeding your group's work. Stress that you expect *each* to be responsible for *51 percent* of the relationship!

Resist any attempts to drag you back into examining past conflicts. Your only concern is improving their future working relationship. Make clear that you don't expect your employees to *like* each other, but you *do* expect them to work with each other, regardless of their likes or dislikes.

After this discussion, become very intolerant of any repetition of the problems. At the first sight of a new outbreak, stop the discussion, calling a recess to a meeting if necessary, and take the two of them outside. Reiterate your point firmly, asking each to acknowledge it to you before resuming the meeting with the rest of the group.

The bickering may continue in spite of your efforts. You may then have to remove (by transferring or even terminating) one or both of the participants. Be prepared to do this even though it may mean the loss of talented individuals.

"MORALE KILLER" MUST BE DEALT WITH, EVEN IF HE DOES GOOD WORK

QUESTION

I am the manager of a department of twenty-five people. My staff are all hardworking, conscientious people, except for one. He's a real morale killer. He's always complaining and making comments like, "We tried that, and it didn't work," or, "They won't let us do that."

He's so negative that he's dragging down the rest of the staff. I don't want to fire him; he does good work. But how do I keep him from hurting the rest of my staff's morale?

ANSWER

First, make sure your employee understands your assessment of both his work and the impact of his behavior. He may have no idea how much harm his conduct causes. Illustrate your complaint with numerous specific examples. Only through such examples will you have a chance to drive your point home.

Having discussed both his work contributions and the impact of his attitude, point out that you must be concerned with the work output of the *entire group,* and that if he does not modify his destructive behavior, his overall usefulness is questionable.

After the meeting, keep an eye out for further incidents and comment on them immediately to amplify your general message. Do this privately. If he acts up in meetings, pass him a note unobtrusively asking him to stop.

Be persistent; one conversation is unlikely to change what is probably well-entrenched behavior.

When it comes to people and their quirks, idiosyncrasies, and personality flaws, the variety seems to be limitless. The manager's aim always remains the same: to keep these human issues from clogging up the workings of their group.

A JUDGMENTAL EMPLOYEE IS UNSURE OF HIS OWN ABILITY

QUESTION

One of my young employees suffers from "judgmentalitis": He's too quick to judge his coworkers. He also has an exceptionally high—sometimes too high—opinion of his own capabilities. He *is* a talented worker who came up quickly through the ranks, but his unforgiving attitude toward others causes disruption and diminishes his value.

I've spoken to him about his attitude, and although his behavior has changed slightly, his outlook has not. I feel he is only altering his behavior to please me, without really believing what I tell him.

Is there any way of helping him to see that empathy is an important skill at the workplace?

ANSWER

Such behavior is often displayed by people who have enjoyed rapid success. Your employee's outstanding skills have led to rapid advancement. Perhaps his advancement was so fast that it left him wondering, deep down, if he can continue to live up to such high expectations. He may be using the shortcomings of his coworkers as a way to reassure himself. As he gains more confidence in his own ability, he's likely to regain a more balanced perspective of his and others' capabilities.

Meanwhile, hammer home to him that his performance now is linked to the performance of the entire group; therefore, he can only excel if the entire group does.

IS A DEFENSIVE EMPLOYEE WORTH THE TROUBLE?

QUESTION

One of my employees is hypersensitive to criticism. He takes every remark I make about his work personally and sulks for days after I gently point out errors. He even takes compliments and turns them into criticism. For example, I remarked recently that a report he had done had been particularly comprehensive, and he responded defensively, "Why, wasn't it supposed to be?"

It's getting so I hate to criticize him because he reacts so defensively. He's a valuable employee, but he's not going to get any better if he doesn't learn to take criticism in stride. What can I do to get through to him on this?

ANSWER

I am afraid I don't have good news for you. In my experience, people with a strong tendency toward defensiveness don't change. If you've tried to reason with your employee without any improvement, you may have a hard-core case on your hands.

I suggest that you accept that he won't change but also resolve that you will continue to comment on his work—compliment him and criticize him—regardless of his defensiveness.

You clearly know the "penalty" that your employee will mete out as a result of such comments. Now, ask yourself, "Is he worth the trouble?" If the answer is yes, set your jaw and continue on. If not, sit down with your employee and explain to him that his work, while good, is not worth the trouble he's causing you and suggest that he look for a job elsewhere.

The worst thing about situations like this is that we won't write off an employee who is causing a lot of trouble without first spending a great deal of energy on trying to fix the problem. Working on losers can be terribly wasteful: The problem employees will get a disproportionate part of the boss's attention to the detriment of the group as a whole, and often for naught.

This is a lesson every manager needs to learn for himself. As a young and inexperienced manager, I spent many months trying to "cure" a lazy employee. I tried everything I could think of. I spent hours talking with him, more hours consulting with fellow managers, and, worst of all, I was constantly thinking about the situation—on and off the job. All this was to no avail; the employee remained lackadaisical. At the same time, I started to miss *other* problems elsewhere. Eventually I came to realize the obvious: I was fighting my noble but losing battle to the detriment of the group's—and therefore my—overall performance.

Much too late, I decided to cut our losses and terminated the person. Only then did I fully realize how much time and energy I had sunk into this situation. It would have been so much more productive if I had devoted it to the healthy part of the group!

MY EMPLOYEE IS BORED WITH ME!

Handling insecure and defensive personalities is hard enough, but things get even more difficult when the manager's own persona is part of the problem.

QUESTION

I am an inexperienced manager, responsible for seven workers. I have a problem with one of them. Whenever I talk with her, she acts extremely bored and disinterested. She's very efficient, but I am still troubled by her lack of enthusiasm. How can I get this person to respond in a more enthusiastic manner?

ANSWER

Your first priority should be your employee's work. Concentrate on that—thoroughly and objectively. Her attitude should be a secondary concern. Keep in mind that as a new supervisor, you are probably overly self-conscious and sensitive, and that your employee may also resent you in your new position. Time will help all of that; as you get settled in your job, the problem may simply go away.

If it doesn't, bring up your concern with your employee, if for no other reason than just to make it more pleasant for the two of you to work together. Since the discussion is likely to be a touchy one, arrange to have it at a time and place where you won't be interrupted.

Start out by telling her that her boredom is obvious and ask her to comment. If she denies that she's disinterested, ask her how she feels about working for you. One way or another, induce her to talk about her views and perceptions of you and how you are doing your job as her boss. Stress that you are interested in doing whatever you can to make your work together more enjoyable.

Be prepared to hear some unpleasant comments about your own conduct; the type of situation you describe often reflects a two-way problem. Don't argue with her when she starts criticizing you. Listen!

A good, frank exchange may help build a foundation for a better—a more productive and more enjoyable—work relationship.

HELP, I JUST DON'T LIKE ONE OF MY EMPLOYEES

QUESTION

I am a middle manager, and I've got a problem. For reasons that aren't clear to me, I just don't like one of my employees.

The man does a good job and he's a valuable employee, so I don't want to lose him. However, as time goes by I become less and less objective about his performance. He picks up on my negative vibrations, and I think he behaves in a way that only exacerbates the situation.

For example, while I don't think I am generally nit-picky when it comes to reports, I find that I examine his with a magnifying glass. Of course, once I do that, I find plenty of things for him to fix. Then, when he does his reports over, they come back *worse* than they were in the first place.

How can I break this chain?

ANSWER

You've made the most difficult and crucial step in coping with this problem when you recognized that your dislike of your employee is clouding your assessment of his work. You couldn't deal with it unless you recognized it. Now you must discipline yourself to handle the situation in a much more rational way.

Work consciously toward putting your evaluation of the employee's performance on an objective basis. Ask yourself exactly what it is that you want from him: what he should accomplish and by when. Then establish a clear understanding of these goals between the two of you and force yourself to concentrate on his work rather than on your personal feelings.

For instance, clarify in your own mind what characteristics a good report should have. Jot these down on a piece of paper and go over them with your employee. Having established such criteria in advance should help him produce reports that meet your approval on the first attempt and eliminate the mutually frustrating cycle of rewrites.

This is the essence of "management by objectives." It should help you concentrate on your employee's accomplishments and keep your feelings about him in check.

IF YOU GIVE IN TO AN EMPLOYEE'S THREATS, YOU'RE SUNK

There are also times when your personal involvement in a conflict becomes more substantive—it's no longer just an issue of likes and dislikes, but a true struggle of wills and personalities.

QUESTION

I am a department manager. Recently one of my employees and I got embroiled in a protracted disagreement involving an organizational matter. He wants to solve it one way, while I am leaning in a different direction. We've had a number of discussions on the matter but can't seem to reach an agreement.

The last time we discussed it, he told me that if I didn't agree to his solution, he would quit. I still don't like his solution, but I have to consider the fact that he'd be hard to replace.

ANSWER

In my view, your employee has already resolved the issue for you. No manager should consider *anything* under a threat! If you give in now, the working relationship between the two of you will be poisoned forever. You will both know that he threatened you and that you gave in, and you'll both anticipate a repeat of that situation every time you sit down to consider a new issue.

Get together with your employee and explain that when he made his threat you had not yet made up your mind on the issue, but he left you no alternative but to proceed with *your* solution. Illustrate the difficulty the two of you would have if you gave in to him. Ask him to put himself in your shoes and imagine how he would cope with such a threat. Stress that, other than his conduct on this issue, you value his contributions, and express the hope that you can both forget the incident.

Ask him to think about it rather than to respond on the spot, and set up a time and a place where he can give you his answer. There is a good chance he'll reappear with an apology. If he does, put the whole situation out of your mind. If he doesn't, part company. This may cause you immediate difficulties, but you'll definitely be better off in the long run.

This situation was one where the writer subsequently let me know what happened. He followed my suggestion and his employee immediately backed away from further conflict, claiming that he had never intended to threaten and that the whole thing was a misunderstanding. In any event, a good working relationship was restored between the two of them.

A SUBORDINATE'S RÉSUMÉ IS ON THE "STREET"

Another kind of incident that will strain the capabilities of any manager involves the loss or potential loss of a valued subordinate. Chances are that you haven't done a wonderful job of managing this individual, so you'll be likely to become defensive. Hard as it is, if you are to remedy the situation now, you *must* rise above your own guilt feelings and concentrate fully on your employee's problem.

QUESTION

I manage a group of product-planning people. I recently heard from a reliable source that one of my best contributors has his résumé out. I was under the impression that this person is happy with his job and feels challenged. He hasn't complained about his raises not being adequate or about anything else.

I feel that my next step must be correct or I will lose him. How should I proceed?

ANSWER

You don't have any alternative but to approach your employee in a straightforward way. Schedule a private meeting and allow enough time to handle what could be a very uncomfortable discussion. Preface your comments with the same statements that you made in your question to me—that is, that you thought he was happy and challenged by his work.

Tell him that you consider him one of your best contributors and that you're puzzled by his apparent interest in leaving. Ask him what might have prompted him to start looking on the outside. Stress very emphatically that your aim is to satisfy his needs so that he will have no reason or desire to look for a change.

Then, after you've made this point, *stop talking* and *start listening*. Remember, your employee was taken by surprise and will probably feel tense. Be patient. Give him time to sort out his thoughts. You are not likely to hear his real reason for wanting to change jobs right away, but eventually he'll tell you.

Then go to work to remedy the cause. Sometimes people put out a résumé merely to assure themselves that they are still valued and desirable. Keep this possibility in mind. Perhaps you've been taking him too much for granted, and he doesn't know how much you appreciate him. If that's the case, you'll need to provide such reassurance and continue to do so.

A manager's output is the output of his team. Easy to say. As the examples in this chapter have indicated, however, it's not so easy to have all members of the team pull together: They are all individuals with their own concerns, sensitivities, and desires. It's up to the manager to deal with these so that the team can go on and win.

WHEN A UNION VOTE TEARS YOUR EMPLOYEES APART

I know of no situation that is more destructive to teamwork and that is a bigger challenge to the manager's ability to pull his employees together than the intrusion of an external force that serves *its* own interests.

This is what happens when a union attempts to get established at a workplace. Fortunately, I have experienced this situation only once, but even that was once too often. It was at one of our plants, almost ten years ago. As always, management mistakes played a role. A number of arbitrary actions by the plant manager upset some of the employees enough to create a receptive environment for the union organizers. What followed were months of nightmare: arguments, turmoil, dissension; an atmosphere in which the work of the plant took a backseat to everything else.

Eventually, the election came. Over eighty percent of the employees voted to reject the unionization attempt. Still, the return to normalcy was slow. The enmities developed in the preceding months took a long time to heal. It only took a few mistakes to get us all into this situation; it took many months of hard work to get us out of it.

QUESTION

Recently a union tried to come into one of our locations. The issue came to an election; out of ninety-six eligible voters, fifty-four voted against and thirty-four voted for the union. I was relieved that the union was voted down, but how do I manage those thirty-four people who were so unhappy that they thought they needed a union to solve their problems?

ANSWER

Your problem may be even more difficult than your question suggests. Typically, during the campaign preceding a union representation election, feelings run very strong and employees with different leanings get highly polarized.

Friends, even relatives, develop strongly antagonistic feelings toward each other. Employees are alienated from their co-workers. When the election is finally over, the losing party often resents the prevailing one.

As a manager, you have two tasks. First, you must help heal the rift so you can again expect collaboration and teamwork from your group. At all costs, avoid punishing the losers. In the presence of the entire group, express a clear willingness to hear about any problems.

Second, you need to find out why a full third of your people felt that they needed a union to represent them. Since communication between your employees and yourself must have been quite poor, it will take more to get your answers than just asking a few questions. Spend a lot of time at it—meet with your employees in small groups, perhaps having coffee with them—and listen to their questions and comments.

After a while a pattern of complaints will start to emerge, and the true problems will begin to stand out. You must then address these. And always, after this, keep the channels of communication open.

7

Teach, Coach, and Look Over Your People's Shoulders

ONE way managers add value is by letting their employees do work that they would otherwise have to do themselves. This is what *delegation* is about. To delegate successfully a manager has to accept, in his heart as well as his mind, that his true output *is* the sum total of the work of his people. His efforts are therefore best directed toward increasing the output (the quantity and value of the work) of his team.

Ultimately, most managers learn to derive pleasure from the accomplishments and successes of their employees. Before they get there, however, obstacles need to be overcome.

NOBODY CAN DO IT LIKE ME!

Most of us got promoted to management jobs because we had excelled as *doers* before. So, we are likely to judge our employees' performance of a task by comparing it to how *we* might have done it. If they don't measure up, the urge is there to grab that task and do it ourselves. After all, we say to ourselves, we can do it better and it's faster that way than if we guide them through the intricacies of the task, laboriously correcting and explaining along the way.

Of course, the trouble with this reasoning is that this way we'll be stuck with doing that task forever!

QUESTION

I have my own company—I am the sole employee. I contract myself out to other companies to write brochures for them. I am well-paid, but I want my company to grow, which means taking on more clients.

My problem is this: I spend a lot of time doing research and other legwork on my projects, as well as all of the editing. In order to find new clients, I have to free up more time by hiring an editor to help out. My fear is that as I do this, I will sacrifice the quality of my work. Any advice?

Is there a manager alive who has not been gripped by such a fear? But you can't succeed as a manager without finding a way to overcome this hang-up.

ANSWER

Even though you are just a one-person business, your problem is similar to that faced by many growing companies. There is no way to expand your enterprise while you continue to do everything. You must learn to bring help aboard—necessary for growth—without letting the quality of your organization's work suffer. This involves a critical balance: If you are too conservative, you lose opportunities. But if you get ahead of yourself, the poor work quality that may result could kill the goose that lays the golden eggs.

The nature of your own work will clearly have to change. You will have to shift some of your time to prospecting for new clients, and as you bring on other employees, such as an editor, you'll have to *train* them in the work style to which your customers have become accustomed.

Then, as your new editor takes over some of the work you used to do, you'll need to *monitor* his or her work. In the beginning, you will have to watch it closely until you are sure that you can maintain the same pride in your editor's work that you did in your own. Remember, now that you manage, your employee's work output is also *your* work output.

If this addition to your company is successful, there will be others. You'll need to devote more and more of your time to such tasks as training, monitoring, and evaluating your employees' work—and that is as it should be.

IT'S A MISTAKE TO LET EMPLOYEES MAKE MISTAKES

Training, monitoring, and *evaluating* are what successful delegation is built on. Or, put another way, to delegate successfully, a manager must become a *teacher* and a *coach*.

The trickiest part in this teaching/coaching process is deciding when and how to let go of the reins. This is an issue that troubles supervisors and employees alike.

One school of thought is expressed by the writer of the next question.

QUESTION
Should I try to prevent my employees from making mistakes? After all, they may learn best through their own mistakes.

ANSWER
A supervisor should do his best to guide his employees in such a way that they learn without making mistakes that would damage an innocent third party—for instance, a customer. Medical schools don't train surgeons by letting them experiment on their own; airlines don't teach pilots by letting them crash planes. They

teach them in such a way that no damage is done to others. If you are an engineering manager, draw on your own experience as an engineer to call your employee's attention to a possible "gotcha" in his design; if you are a sales manager, visit some of your junior salespersons' accounts and satisfy yourself that service and relationships are as they should be.

Clearly, it is a lot more difficult to teach our employees in this fashion. It places a greater burden on the supervisor, forcing him to look over the employee's shoulder, to guide his hand and be ready to interject himself if major calamities threaten. But it is all part of the supervisor/teacher's job.

People who argue in favor of letting an employee loose under the guise of "letting him learn from his own mistakes" are letting others pay the price of the schooling.

THE RIGHT TO FLY "SOLO" MUST BE EARNED

Beyond this idea of "letting them learn from their own mistakes," managers and employees alike frequently have problems deciding how soon to let go, how much needs to be checked, and for how long.

The key to finding the right answer for a given situation is to keep in mind that even after the manager/teacher has taught his employee/pupil a certain skill, the quality of the resulting work remains the responsibility of the manager. So, monitoring, checking, evaluating—with sufficient rigor to insure that the results are satisfactory—must go on until it can be proven that the need for them no longer exists. (Remember, surgeons and pilots have to pass rigorous tests before they are permitted to be on their own.)

QUESTION

As the supervisor of five people, I double-check their work to be certain our projects are completed accurately and on schedule. I often find the quality of their work inferior—their work standards just don't measure up to mine. I find this situation very stressful, and I resent having to play detective and to remind my employees of deadlines. What do you suggest?

QUESTION

Recently I started working in a library. My boss is a kind lady. Since I am new on the job, she is watching me closely and tries to help me out. In the beginning, I really appreciated her help. Now that I have become familiar with the work, it makes me nervous that she hovers over me. In fact, her presence causes me to make mistakes that I don't commit when she is not around. What should I do?

QUESTION

I report to an assistant manager who finds *everything* I do wrong! I have tried to talk to her to find out what bothers her, but to no avail. By now, everyone watches over me and checks everything I do. It drives me crazy! What can I do about it?

ANSWER

The quality of the work output of a group is the responsibility of its manager. So, a manager who takes his or her job seriously will check the work of the group *as much as necessary*. This is not "playing detective" and is not anything that a manager should resent doing—it's part of the job!

How much to check and what to do when an employee's work contains errors are other matters. When a person is new on the job, he or she needs to be trained. This, too, is the responsibility of the manager; this, too, is part of the job. Even after training has taken place, the skills learned will not be thoroughly absorbed for a while, so checking and reinforcing is appropriate.

With time and practice on the job the employee learns, and a good supervisor will ease up, but without letting go completely. Maybe he'll check every fourth piece of work, or maybe he'll check only the particularly tricky ones, but check he must for quite some time, keeping in mind that he remains forever responsible for the quality of the employee's work.

It's understandable if the employee is impatient to be permitted to "fly solo" on his job—after all, that is a compliment to his capabilities and a sign that he has arrived. But that condition has to be earned.

Let me suggest this to the employee anxious to be left to his or her own devices: Ask for a meeting with your boss. Express your desire to perform your job without having your work constantly checked. Ask for a set of conditions which, if met, would earn you your "license" to operate independently.

These could be, for instance, to produce some amount of work without any errors, or to make a customer presentation with your boss present but only watching, or to demonstrate your knowledge of the task at hand by undertaking to train a new employee yourself.

Then, go to work trying to meet those conditions.

HOW MANY WORKERS SHOULD A MANAGER SUPERVISE?

One built-in enemy of proper delegation is for a manager to have *too many* or *too few* workers under him. The wrong number of employees will *force* a manager into inappropriate activities. Give a manager too few employees, and he'll needlessly meddle with their work—not having anything else to occupy him. Go overboard in the other direction, and the manager will be stretched so thin he won't be able to check on their work at all.

QUESTION

I am a middle manager, and I already have four people working for me. In a recent reorganization, my boss told me that I'll have to supervise two more individuals, who are involved in quite a different set of activities than the others I already supervise. My current employees occupy me full-time, and if I stretch myself further, the quality of my work as a manager will suffer. Is there a way to decide if a person's supervisory load is too much or just right?

ANSWER

There is no set number of employees that is just right. The number of workers a manager can supervise depends on *their* experience level. If they are all very experienced, the manager can supervise more of them than if they are brand-new to their current assignments.

I think the minimum number of employees a full-time manager should have under his or her supervision is six; the maximum is twelve or so. Managing four should not tax a full-time supervisor too much under any circumstances. If you feel overloaded, you may need to reevaluate how you supervise. Perhaps you should introduce more systematic communication channels and methods of monitoring the work of your employees.

In fact, organizations that find themselves in a more competitive environment (and today there are a lot of those . . . Intel being one, too!) find that having too many layers of management is a burden. It costs more, of course, but each additional layer of management also slows the responsiveness of the organization: Information has to travel longer and decision making is more cumbersome. Consequently, there is a current trend toward flattening the management hierarchy. For instance, in the old scheme of things, a department head may have had three groups under his supervision, with each group supervisor looking after three or four employees' work. If the employees are well trained and experienced, this same department can be managed by the department head alone supervising the activities of the entire group of nine to twelve employees. The main benefit of this arrangement is that the manager is now in direct contact with each employee doing the work; hence he can respond to their problems more immediately and effectively.

Under such conditions, the manager will have far less opportunity to take over the work of his employees and do it himself—he will be too busy managing their work.

HE WANTS YOUR JOB

You have developed your employees well through the years; you trained, monitored, and evaluated them—and now you find yourself with a new problem, perhaps one that you secretly feared all along.

QUESTION

How do you deal with an assistant who wants your job? That's my situation. To be fair, my assistant is hardworking, bright, and very talented. He's also extremely ambitious—it's pretty clear he wants my job, and soon. I don't really want to lose him; he's too valuable to our department.

But I have no intention of giving up my job to him. Should I load on the assignments and try to keep him too busy to be ambitious? Or should I find a way to fire him?

ANSWER

Fire him? Banish the very thought! You are one lucky manager. Most of us in the business world would give an eyetooth to have a hardworking, bright, talented, and ambitious second-in-command working for us.

To resolve your immediate problem, sit down with him and discuss how you can use him more while he is in your group. For instance, are there projects he could undertake on your behalf? Has *he* trained someone to take *his* job if he were to move on?

And most importantly, explore career options other than your own job; look for ways of rounding him out and providing him with varied experiences that would enable him to become a candidate for a number of higher positions in the company, not just yours.

Many managers are overlooked for promotion themselves because they did not develop a successor who could take over their job. So, cherish your assistant; he is an asset to you and your organization, and key to your own further career growth.

8

High Expectations and a Bit of Zest Get Results

IT never ceases to amaze me how much difference there can be between the performance of groups of people who have the same level of skills—but have different supervisors! It seems that besides superior knowledge, good managers have an almost magical ability to infuse their subordinates with energy and drive to perform.

I say "almost magical" for a reason. The ability is hard to analyze, and if it can't be analyzed, it can't be taught. (Remember: Copying a successful manager's mannerisms won't do it!) But I've watched managers who are good at it, and I've made a few observations.

Managers who can successfully mobilize their workers set *high expectations* for them. Not ridiculously high—just high enough to get their competitive juices flowing. This is one reason why a manager should know a good bit about the work being performed in his or her group: to be able to set expectations at the *right level*.

A particular situation comes to mind. A manager at Intel took over a manufacturing group whose performance had been mediocre for some time. In the first two months he went around and spent a lot of time talking with his people. His message was that the previous standards of performance were no longer good enough—competition in the marketplace had gotten tougher. Then he outlined, in detail, the new levels of work performance he needed from each of his subgroups. He had done his homework: The new standards were harder than the previous ones, but only by a reasonable step, one that could be achieved, albeit not easily. A new level of energy spread through his group as they accepted the challenge of these new goals. Performance improved, eventually reaching the new levels across the board.

Sounds easy? It isn't. It's not only hard to figure out at the start what we really want, but also nothing will be accomplished unless the desired goal is presented to the employees in terms they can fully understand. Setting and communicating the right expectations is the most important tool a manager has for imparting that elusive drive to the people he supervises.

HOW DO I PUSH HER TO WORK HARDER?

QUESTION

I am an accounting supervisor. My problem involves managing a new employee, a woman who is about ten years older than I am. She does exactly what I tell her to do—nothing more. For instance, she sends out all the bills she is supposed to, but when she is done she will sit around waiting for someone to give her something to do even though piles of unopened envelopes may be stacked on the next desk. I have to spend considerable energy to push her to work harder. What should I do?

ANSWER

Many new employees hesitate to go beyond specific instructions for fear of doing the wrong thing. You need to discuss with your employee not just the specific job requirements but also your expectations on a broader scale. Explain to her that you regard her as a member of the office team and that you expect her to look around and help out whoever is behind—the same as you would expect the others to do for her if she needed help. Stress that you expect her to keep her eyes open and show initiative in finding such situations.

As she becomes more comfortable with her duties, she'll get a "feel" for what she can do over and above them in order to meet your broader expectations. This will not happen overnight, but if you have clearly communicated an increased level of expectation, it will eventually result in improved performance.

And forget about her age. She is your employee and you are responsible for her work. Her age is irrelevant.

TELL HIM FRANKLY WHAT YOU EXPECT

QUESTION

I own a small company. I have a hard time finding qualified employees who are willing to work for me, given the work conditions I offer. I have finally found an employee who is quite knowledgeable and who *can* do a good job—when he wants to. My problem is that I can't get him to stop goofing off. He is constantly socializing instead of working.

I have promised him pay increases tied to an increase in his productivity, but that hasn't helped. I recently overheard him complaining to his coworkers, "The boss never notices any extra work that we do, but she always notices when we take five minutes of break time."

I'd really like to resolve this conflict. Although I never noticed any extra work from him, I was contemplating praising him for extra effort, hoping that it would encourage him to work harder.

Is that a good idea?

ANSWER

Not at all! The problem between the two of you is that each of you has very different expectations of what your employee should be doing. You'll lose any chance you have to resolve the conflict the minute you give him phony praise. The gap in expectations can only be closed by some frank, thorough, and factual discussions between the two of you.

Take the initiative: Set up a meeting with your employee and present him with a detailed look at his performance compared to your expectations. Base this discussion on *work output,* not on *time spent* working.

Give him a written summary of your evaluation and expectations and ask him to return with his response after he's had a chance to think it over. (To keep it simple, he can mark up your evaluation with his comments.) Keep in mind that unless the two of you can agree on what he has been doing and what he can be expected to do, you will forever be locked in a conflict that's bound to have an undesirable outcome. And have an open mind; after all, it is possible that your expectations are unrealistic.

IT'S OK TO ENJOY YOURSELF AT WORK

Zest is a key ingredient that's inevitably present in groups with high energy and drive. Small wonder, if you think about it: We spend a major part of our lives at work. It's certainly a lot easier to sustain a high level of commitment to it if we enjoy the work environment.

So, do everything you can to enjoy *yourself* at work and to permit *your employees* to do so as well. Just keep in mind while you are having fun: It *is* a place of work! The fun part should support the work part, not detract from it.

Here are a few pointers:

- Celebrate *achievements,* not the fact that it's Friday! Try to provide as many interim milestones as you can, and supplant the long-term drive toward reaching a major result with a series of shorter steps. Then, use the occasions when one of these is achieved as events to be noted, even in a small way.
- Don't let any celebration become a distraction to others who work. (I remember one time when an entire engineering organization was shut down because the computer operators were celebrating some big event and no one was manning the machines!)

- Poke gentle fun at each other, including your boss (it's good for him—he shouldn't be too serious!).
- Compete—with other departments or groups—but *keep it light!*

EMPLOYEE-OF-THE-MONTH KNOWS SOMEBODY CARES

QUESTION

I work for a company where each month an employee is chosen as "Employee of the Month." The winner receives a certificate for dinner for two and a plaque with his or her name engraved on it. I assume this is an incentive to make people work harder. Does it work?

ANSWER

I feel that the key element in arrangements like this is that they recognize good performance. The fact that an employee gets chosen each month for his or her performance says to *all* employees that somebody cares about their work, evaluates it, and provides feedback.

We may never be able to prove that this motivates people, but I am convinced that it does. Furthermore, I think it injects a bit of celebration into the work environment and makes it more fun for everybody. So I strongly agree that a practice like this is useful, and recommend it—in whatever version your budget allows.

OFFICE COMPETITION NEEDS A TOUCH OF HUMOR

As I said, competition at the workplace must be kept light. This is what it can be like if the manager gets carried away with the competitive element alone.

QUESTION

My boss has set up a demoralizing competitive arena in our office. He thinks that he can enhance a worker's performance by praising one over another; I guess he hopes that we'll all try to outdo one another and that our productivity will increase. He even goes so far as to manipulate the work statistics of one worker favorably to make another worker look bad.

This is a no-win situation. All of us who work together are getting nervous. Is there anything we can do?

ANSWER

If competition is to be a positive experience, it should be fair and a bit lighthearted. It sounds like yours is neither. My suggestion is that instead of trying to induce your boss to eliminate competition, you should attempt to convince him to change the manner in which he sets it up.

Catch your boss privately and discuss the whole issue with him. Point out specifics where statistics were distorted, and ask that the competition should be made to take place under meticulously fair rules. Suggest ways to focus on the winners and to introduce some levity and a sense of sportsmanship. For example, you may help your boss devise a homemade trophy that could sit on the desk of the winner of the week and migrate to the next winner with a little ceremony. In this way, the need for good performance can be emphasized without damaging everyone's morale.

Having said all this, I have my doubts if this particular boss is capable or willing to change.

VARIETY CAN ADD "SPICE" TO WORK

But even when the manager's expectations are clearly set and the workplace is stimulating, any job can become tedious after a while. It is harder and harder to create and sustain energy and drive if people have to do the same job forever.

Rotating people and letting them work in different assignments is an excellent way to keep a person's work interesting. In addition, it serves to enrich and develop the employees' skills. It's a pity that it isn't practiced more broadly.

QUESTION

I work for a nonprofit summer camp for elementary school children. We have about thirty employees, including counselors and staff, each of whom are paid the same monthly honorarium. We are all volunteers and work for less than normal pay to keep operating costs down. The problem is that some jobs are harder than others; staff jobs especially demand hard, tedious work. As a result, after a few weeks, staff personnel become less motivated than counselors. We can't afford to pay anyone extra, and our efforts to provide additional recognition to staff personnel have not accomplished much. What could we do to improve this situation?

ANSWER

Your best bet is to rotate your employees through all the jobs. For instance, let counselors and camp staff alternate assignments each week or two. This would break the monotony and make everybody's job more interesting. This seems both fair and practical, and it would also offer a wider experience base to each person.

9

Praise or Criticism—
Both Needed, Neither Easy

Could *you* have written this?

I HATE GIVING CRITICISM

QUESTION

There's nothing I hate more at work than giving criticism—
whether it's in the context of a formal performance appraisal or
casual conversation over coffee. But since I'm a manager (of a
clothing store), I have to criticize my fellow employees. How can
I make the experience easier for myself and, at the same time,
helpful to the employee and still get the results I want?

In my experience, most managers could have written this letter.
Let's go another step. Could you have written *this?*

MY BOSS DOESN'T GIVE ME FEEDBACK

QUESTION

I run a branch office for my company. My problem is that I don't get any feedback from my boss unless something goes wrong. I assume when I don't hear from her that I'm doing okay, but I don't like making assumptions about my performance.

I've tried to stimulate discussions about my performance with her, but she just doesn't seem to understand. What can I do to get her to give me the feedback I need?

Since you are also an employee yourself, as most managers are, you probably could have written this letter too. In fact, the two grievances are closely related: It *is* hard to make comments evaluating another's work. Most managers are less qualified to handle this part of their job than any other.

I'll go a step further. The reluctance to give feedback is the most common shortcoming people in supervisory work have. I think a part of the problem is that by committing ourselves to a position we bosses take some risk. What if we criticize something our employee has done—and we turn out to be wrong? We'll be in for a big argument, hurt feelings, may even have to retract our comment. Isn't it safer to say nothing?

It's even worse when it comes to compliments. What if we give misplaced praise? What if the job our employee has done *isn't* as good as it looks? He certainly won't argue with us but won't he go off laughing at our naïveté? It's again safer to say nothing.

Yet giving feedback—criticizing and praising—is the most important tool of the managing trade. It's through feedback that we'll nudge our employees in the right direction, set and modify their expectations, and coax them along toward improved performance. Hard as it may be, we *must* criticize and we *must* praise.

My answer to the first writer:

ANSWER

Remind yourself frequently that your job is *not to criticize* your employees but to *critique* their work. You are there to get the best performance from them in the interest of your department or company. Evaluating their work and offering constructive comments on how they can improve is a major tool in achieving that performance.

Having said this, I must caution you that it will never be easy. The temptation will always be to equivocate, to take the easy way out. Steel yourself to be truthful and consistent—not only because that's the right way, but because in the long run that's also the most effective.

Easier said than done, I agree.

To this day, I often find myself guilty of *not* expressing how I feel about something an employee has done, or at least, not in a timely fashion. Sometimes I catch myself an hour or so later muttering, "I should have told him that was no way to handle that situation . . ." Then I take myself in hand, go down the hall or reach for the telephone, and tell the person. "I should have told you right then but as I've thought about it, it's become even clearer that what you did was not right . . ."

I have the exact same problem with compliments. There is an old, old handwritten sign I posted on the wall over my desk that says, "Say something nice!" As I talk on the telephone or read memos and reports, many times this sign has prompted me to express what I already felt but might have kept to myself.

The employee has a role to play in this, too. He or she can try prompting the boss by asking for comments when a task is completed

("Is this how you wanted it done?"). I answered the second writer along this line.

ANSWER

Not only do you need feedback regarding your work, you are entitled to it. The question is, how to get it.

Since you can't get feedback without contact, your first move should be to set up regular routine get-togethers with your boss. Face-to-face meetings would be the best, but even telephone contact may do the job if you are not at the same physical location. These encounters should be prearranged so they are convenient for your boss and she can allot sufficient time—don't try to drop in or just give her a casual call. Set up the visit or call in advance, telling her that you need to discuss your project (your customers, or whatever) with her.

Send her a note listing the subjects you intend to discuss. Your supervisor may feel uncomfortable discussing your performance or giving you feedback, but she'll be ready and willing to discuss the details of your work.

Make such meetings a predictable routine. Schedule them yourself, prepare for them thoroughly, concentrating on areas where you are really likely to benefit from your boss's advice and judgment.

If you find the meetings productive, I'm certain your boss will also, and after a while she won't resist them. And, in the course of these meetings, you'll get the feedback you need.

WHEN YOU CRITICIZE AN EMPLOYEE TOO HARSHLY

Even when we are put into the role of evaluators we are still imperfect human beings ourselves. We have our own emotions and moods that we invariably bring into the fray.

QUESTION

One of my best employees just finished a major project. She did an excellent job, but when she showed me her finished work the first thing I noticed was an error. I pointed this out to her in an annoyed manner and then went on to study the rest of her work, which was excellent.

Later on, I told her that she did a very good job, but my first reaction ruined the impact of my compliments. She's been very upset and angry with me ever since, and is even considering quitting, in spite of the fact that I got her a nice bonus for the job she did on the project. How can I salvage this situation?

ANSWER

When your employee showed you her work, she was probably anxiously awaiting your reaction. Your first statement devastated her. In one second you deflated the pride she had in her report. In her mind you were reacting to the whole job—even if in *your* mind it was not so. You were clearly insensitive to the impact your opening comment would have on her.

Unfortunately you can't replay that scene. The only thing you can do is to explain the context in which you made your comment and apologize for your insensitivity.

Because this is clearly an emotional subject for her (and probably for you), I suggest that you put your explanation and apology in writing. She'll find it easier to consider what you have to say while reading your letter in private rather than trying to cope with your explanation while facing you. Don't be defensive—after all, you too are only human.

She made an error in her work and you have committed one in yours. You should have seen her error in the proper perspective, and now you have to ask her to be understanding of your error. I'll lay odds she will be.

Comments about performance don't even have to be harsh to be devastating. Lack of specifics is at least as destructive. The very first performance evaluation I ever got followed my first six months of work, in which I thought I did some worthwhile things. The review didn't deal with these things at all; instead it rated my "attitude," "initiative," "collaborative tendencies," etc., on a numerical scale, and even this wasn't as positive as I expected. I was crushed with disappointment.

I've done a lot of reviewing since that time, and I'm something of a connoisseur on the subject. I've written articles on it and have been teaching a "how-to" course to fellow managers for years. Yet hardly a year goes by that I don't botch up at least one of my employees' reviews in some way, causing them similar disappointment.

Here are a couple of recent examples. Although one of my fundamental principles is that a performance review should always help the employee improve his or her performance, I was so carried away recently complimenting one employee that, at the end of the review, he just looked at me and asked, "Do you really mean to say that I am perfect?" It turns out that there wasn't one single idea in the entire review that could have been helpful to this person in his future work. Once he reminded me and I overcame my embarrassment, I could easily come up with areas where he could improve on his performance, outstanding as it was.

In another case, in analyzing the performance of another individual—a good performer—I accentuated the problem areas way out of proportion. After I gave him his review, he went over the written performance review with highlighting pens. He highlighted the negative comments in blue and the positive ones in yellow. Then he returned and asked me to sum up how I felt about his performance, overall. When I told him that I was very satisfied, he took out the two typewritten sheets and showed them to me: I was looking at a sea of blue ink with an occasional yellow spot appearing here and there!

If ordinary evaluation, criticism, and praise are hard to give, there are situations where even more determination and judgment are required. Here are two.

THERE'S NO PLACE FOR "CHARADES" IN A REVIEW

QUESTION

I supervise a relatively new employee. Another manager hired him and I "inherited" him when I succeeded this manager in his job.

The problem is, the employee is not working out and, in my judgment, never will. I'm supposed to give him an interim performance appraisal—a kind of probationary review. Should I tell him that I think he'll never make it here, or should I encourage him to do better even though I *know* it won't work?

ANSWER

If you are as sure of your conclusion as you sound, you *should* tell your employee exactly how you feel. Doing anything else would be a game of charades that he is bound to lose whether he deserves to or not.

BRIGHT AND AMBITIOUS BUT FORGETFUL AND LATE

QUESTION

One of my employees presents me with a real dilemma. She's bright, ambitious, energetic, and imaginative, showing great potential. But she makes far too many errors in her work, misses deadlines, forgets meetings, and is often late for work. She always has a perfectly good reason for her errors, tardiness, and forgetfulness. The excuses are always valid; there are just so very many of them. How should I handle the situation?

ANSWER

Stop listening to the excuses. You must emphatically and energetically convince your employee that she is responsible for *results*, period. As long as you are enticed into listening to excuses, she will devote her bright mind, energy, and imagination to inventing them.

When she is truly convinced that only results matter, she'll apply these same attributes to her work. Encourage her to allow extra time and schedule it as "slack" in her projects, and to use her calendar meticulously so as to prevent all those unforeseen events from interfering with her work.

A change like this won't come easily, so dig in for the long process of restructuring the individual's values. But when you succeed, you'll have the satisfaction of transforming a good employee into a superior one.

Ideally, we should evaluate our employees' work in two ways: in an ongoing, informal process, and also in a periodic (e.g., annual) and formal manner.

We should give feedback continually as we observe our employees' work—when they do something noteworthy, good or bad, or whenever they do something that reveals that they have mastered a new skill. Such ongoing commentary should be informal and related to the specifics of the moment.

For example, if your secretary handles a difficult assignment well, tell her that you appreciate what she did, pointing out specifically what you liked about it. If an employee solves a customer's problem by doing something extra, compliment him or her on the initiative right then and there.

By contrast, the periodic major performance review should take a broader perspective. It should look at the employee's performance over a year's time. It should describe broader trends and tendencies and give guidance that not only will teach the employee how to do a particular aspect of his job better, but will also improve his performance over a long period of time. For example, you may find that an employee just doesn't understand the products of your firm well enough, and therefore his or her performance tends toward superficiality. In such a case you may suggest a course of action that, over time, will greatly improve the employee's knowledge (send him or her to seminars? assign reading material?). Or you may find that your employee is not well suited to the job by his or her temperament. A review is a good forum in which to examine possible new assignments that may better match his or her skills or personality.

The two types of feedback are not substitutes for each other; they should be complementary.

A few observations about formal performance reviews:

A REVIEW SHOULD BE IN WRITING

QUESTION

I fully believe in the importance of well-executed performance reviews, but I have trouble with my company's requirement that these reviews be written as well as delivered verbally. Aside from the fact that writing them is time-consuming and, in my view, represents a needless bureaucratic burden, having to commit my comments and criticisms to paper inhibits me.

Anybody will be able to read those comments, even years from now. I am not as inclined to be totally straight, as I would be if I could just tell my subordinates what I think. Do you feel written reviews are really necessary?

ANSWER

I absolutely do. For one thing, I believe that an employee's review should always be validated and approved by two involved yet somewhat removed individuals—the boss's supervisor and a representative of the human resources organization. They can only do that if they have a written review to work with.

But even more importantly, a written review is the only tool we have to make sure that verbal comments are not overly ambiguous. Let's face it, most bosses are loath to give difficult messages. When faced with the need to look an employee in the eyes and tell him something that will hurt, many managers will water down the message. The written review is a good way for them to discipline themselves to deliver the message as it was intended.

LATE REVIEWS ARE DISRESPECTFUL

QUESTION

I work for a start-up company in Silicon Valley. I have been with the company a little over three years. For the past two years, my review has been late (my raise, too!). Last year it was several months late.

I am not the only employee receiving this treatment, either. The company has between three hundred and four hundred employees and has been profitable during the entire three years. I have spoken with my boss about my review, and he tells me it will be completed soon but that, at the moment, he is too busy. I have also brought the matter to the attention of my boss's boss, who said it wasn't his responsibility and denies he can do anything to get my review done.

I find this situation very frustrating and demotivating. Do you have any suggestions?

ANSWER

Let me start my answer by first coming clean. At the time I write this, I too am late with the reviews of several of my people—although only by several weeks, not several months. Also, when I get around to giving them, any pay raises will be made retroactive to the original due date. But still, I am late.

Having confessed this, I must add that such tardiness represents a terribly sloppy managerial practice. By putting a review behind other matters, we say, in effect, that evaluating our employees isn't as important as other things. And that's plain wrong.

Unfortunately, I am not sure there is much you can do about your predicament. You took up the matter with both your boss and his boss (whose answer—washing his hands of responsibility altogether—was pitiful). There is only one avenue left for you to explore: the human resources organization. In most companies, it is the guardian of the review process, and it may get after your boss in earnest. However, I am dubious that it will, since this practice seems to be more a pattern than an isolated incident at your place of work.

You may just have to accept this practice as one of the real-life liabilities of your company that may never change. You can live with it or you may want to count it among whatever other reasons you may have that push you toward seeking a change of employers.

WHAT IF A REVIEW IS REBUTTED?

QUESTION

One of my employees strongly disagreed with my last performance review of him. In fact, he wrote me a lengthy rebuttal, challenging several of my points. Should I change my review of him now?

ANSWER

If your employee brought new information or new insights to his review, something that you now agree with after reading his rebuttal, by all means change it. The review should represent your best insight and judgment, and if you find that you erred, you should correct yourself.

On the other hand, if after reading his rebuttal you still feel the same way, stick to your guns. Talk with your employee. Try to convince him of the validity of your observations. But if you don't succeed, your judgment stands, and your review should stay as written.

You are the boss—you get paid to render a judgment of your employee's performance. I do think it would be fair and considerate to file his rebuttal along with your review, maybe with an annotation that says that, after having considered the rebuttal, you still feel your original review is correct.

CAN A BOSS LOWER A PERFORMANCE RATING TO SAVE MONEY?

The formal review often forms the basis for merit raises. While money and reviews are generally related, the connection between the two can become distorted.

QUESTION

My boss recently gave a review with low ratings to one of my coworkers. When confronted by the employee, he agreed that the review did not accurately represent the employee's performance and implied that the reason for the negative ratings was his need to keep down his operating costs. Was this the right thing to do?

ANSWER

Absolutely not. The employee's rating should be determined by his or her performance alone. No supervisor should ever distort an employee's performance rating because of budgetary constraints. Supervisors usually have a salary budget that they can apportion among their employees based on performance. If the budget is low, all employees should get a proportionately lower raise than if the budget were higher. There is no reason to tinker with performance ratings.

WHEN DO I ASK FOR A RAISE?

QUESTION

I've worked very diligently for over a year. I really feel that I deserve a raise, but I don't want to come right out and ask for it. I think my boss should recognize that I deserve one. What's the right time to ask for a raise?

ANSWER

My advice is, wait a while. Give your boss a chance to get his or her act together—your review may be on its way, just late. Don't ruin his (and your own) pleasure by asking for what is already coming down the pike.

If another month or two passes and there is still no word, ask for a meeting with your boss. In it, ask him to review your performance. If he gives you a satisfactory appraisal, then raise the issue of your compensation. But be sure to maintain an approach where both you and your boss can emerge as "winners": Ask, don't demand, and accept a delay if your request isn't dealt with on the spot.

REVIEWS ARE FREE

Lack of a raise budget should *not* be used as a reason to withhold performance evaluations.

QUESTION

I've been employed by a nonprofit organization on a part-time basis for a year and a half. I was offered the job with what I considered to be a more than adequate hourly wage. However, since I started to work at this agency, I have yet to be reviewed or offered a raise. I, would like to know where I stand. I've mentioned my interest in being reviewed to both my immediate supervisor and the board president, with no effect. The only response I've received is that since the organization is a nonprofit one, raises are not budgeted every year. But reviews are free!

ANSWER

I could not agree more. Reviews *are* free; skipping them is expensive, in terms of morale, motivation, and performance.

When in recent years the semiconductor business went into a deep recession, Intel found that it had to delay its merit-raise program. We debated for a while whether or not we should also delay the performance reviews to which the merit raises are customarily tied. Even though our managers and supervisors were extremely busy in this time period trying to cope with the difficult business conditions, we decided that it was important to go ahead with the performance reviews—despite the lack of raises. Our reason was that our employees needed to be told how they were doing, where they stood, and how they could improve, as much or more than ever.

10

Firing: Hard to Do; Harder to Do Right

HAVE you ever been fired? I have. Even though it was thirty years ago, I still vividly remember the humiliation, the feeling of helplessness, the anger. I recall a sense of, "No! This can't be happening to me!" I recall a feeling of shame—without having done anything to be ashamed about. It was awful.

Have you ever fired anyone? I have. That's not a wonderful experience, either. I remember agonizing over the decision for weeks—questioning, is it right? have I tried everything? I remember the anxiety I felt as I went to meet the employee; I had stage fright. And I remember the look of hurt, the anger in his eyes. This, too, was awful.

Terminating an employee for cause—firing him or her—is a harsh act. It is the ultimate disciplinary action. It obviously hurts the employee most, but it's not easy on those who carry it out, either.

IS IT FAIR TO FIRE AN INCOMPETENT?

Is it really fair to fire a person for nonperformance? After all, the company put him in the job he can't do. Should we really punish the employee for something that is the fault of the company?

QUESTION

I have a senior technician who just can't cut it. I have tried everything to train and motivate him, but he continues to botch up his assignments and drags our whole group with him. I would have fired him a long time ago but I feel guilty—after all, I hired him into the job. Now I see that I shouldn't have; but I did, and I am afraid that it's not fair to punish him for my mistake.

ANSWER

Whether such an action is fair or not depends on whom we have in mind. You are concerned about being fair to the employee. You also have to consider other parties. For instance, what about the employee's coworkers, who may have to carry an extra workload because the person in question is not performing?

You should also consider customers who suffer because of the poor quality of this person's work. Add to this shareholders, whose interest is clearly not being served by a nonperformer, and the question of fairness takes on an entirely different outlook. You may have made a bad selection, but how long should you punish coworkers, customers, and your company's shareholders for this error?

In my view, fairness demands that nonperformers be removed from their positions after all reasonable attempts to elicit satisfactory performance from them have failed. That's the only way you can be fair to all parties involved.

If you have difficulty seeing this point, picture yourself on the receiving end of the services of, let's say, an airline maintenance worker who is incompetent. Is it fair to fire him? Shouldn't the question be, is it fair to you, the traveler, to let him stay in his job?

Once the point is reached where a person must be fired, figuring out the right way to do it is very important. In my experience, terminations are rarely done well. Most managers find them very difficult to carry out so they put them off far too long and then do them in a big hurry, as if to make up for lost time.

One of my coworkers always does these things effectively and, at the same time, in a humane fashion. He takes a great deal of time and starts on the process early. He freely discusses his dissatisfaction with the employee in question and lets him know that in his view the outcome will probably be termination. Since he starts early enough and since he is frank with his employee, the two of them can put a transition plan into effect. The employee has time to look for another job, and when he finds one he is permitted to resign. There is no bitterness—yet an unsatisfactory performer is terminated just the same.

HONESTY IS THE MOST EXPEDIENT COURSE

All this highlights the key ingredient for approaching the difficult job of firing someone in the right way: honesty—with yourself and with the employee.

QUESTION

I was terminated from an electronics firm about six months ago. The manager of the firm refused to give a detailed explanation. There were no obvious reasons for my termination; in fact, he was about to interview me for a supervisory position. Don't I even have a right to an explanation?

QUESTION

Recently I was fired from a job for reasons that were trumped up and ridiculous. In essence, they added up to incompetence. Just a few days ago I got a telephone call from my former boss asking me if I would like to return to work. I liked my job, so I said yes. Should I have asked for a better explanation, perhaps in writing, when I was fired? Should I ask now why I am being rehired?

ANSWER

Both of these questions illustrate how hard it is to confront another person and deal with this difficult issue in an honest and straightforward fashion.

It seems that these supervisors chose to handle the unpleasant task of telling their employees the bad news in ways that were easiest for themselves. One decided to provide no explanation, figuring that then there would be nothing to argue about. The other may have been trying to justify the termination with hard, specific facts that would be difficult to refute but which apparently were not true.

In both cases, employees were left bewildered and frustrated. What's more, people who are fired like this frequently get even angrier as time passes. They run through the circumstances of their termination in their head over and over, and find that the reasons make less and less sense. As the saying goes, honesty would really have been the best course.

As to what the two of you should do now:

To the *first writer:* While you are certainly entitled to an honest explanation, I'm dubious that you'll get it at this late stage. I don't think your ex-boss will be eager to return to a difficult situation that he or she considers closed. Demands for explanation will only get you a terse, uninformative reply. It's just too late to go back and reopen the issue.

To the *second writer:* You have a better chance to get the true story, since you are going back to work at the same place. Arrange for a meeting with your boss. Explain that you'd like to learn from this incident and ask him to explain, in detail and from the beginning, what happened and why. Keep asking questions about why he chose to terminate you, stressing that your intent is to learn from this and to improve your future performance. While I doubt that you'll get a coherent explanation, you probably will learn something from this exchange.

THE CAUSE OF FIRING ISN'T ANYONE ELSE'S BUSINESS

> While I firmly believe in dealing openly with the reasons for a termination, I feel that *confidentiality* is equally important.

QUESTION

My friend was fired from our company two months ago for sitting on unfinished work for a long time. More recently, another coworker was dismissed for the same reason.

When a person gets fired, shouldn't the situation, including the reason for firing him, be brought to the attention of the other employees? This would reduce the likelihood that the same mistake will be repeated.

ANSWER

I think an employee's performance evaluation, particularly when it involves disciplinary action, should be treated as a highly confidential matter. It's the business of the employee and the company—it concerns nobody else.

You are right, however, in wanting to learn from other people's mistakes. It's up to your boss to train you so you don't have to learn on your own what others have already discovered through their errors; it's also his job to communicate expected standards of performance. For example, if he sees an employee procrastinating on a project, he should discuss this with him or her long before it becomes a reason for dismissal.

Standards of performance can, and should be, communicated, but this must be done without violating the employee's right to privacy.

BETWEEN A ROCK AND A HARD PLACE

Being fired can cast a long shadow across a person's career. No manager wants to hire a "bad apple," and certainly, having been discharged for cause will raise a prominent red flag. An employee who's been fired has to carry an extra handicap for a while—until he can build up a good track record that outweighs the negative episode. It's not surprising that employees are tempted to bury past problems.

QUESTION

Recently my twenty-five-year-old son was fired for stealing. He claims he is totally innocent. The incident involved his handing over a cash deposit to another employee. He neglected to get a receipt, and the cash disappeared. The other employee was terminated also.

How can he get another job? He doesn't want to lie but if he says that he was fired, he'll never be selected. Seems like he's between a rock and a hard place!

ANSWER

He certainly is. I sympathize with your son's difficulties, but I would strongly urge him *not* to lie, no matter how hard it will be for him to get another job. He made a mistake of one kind or another; he must face the consequences. It's better to face them now than to look for an easier way—and build a life and a career on a lie, forever living in constant fear of discovery.

MAKE PEACE WITH YOUR ROLE IN YOUR PAST

Hiding the past doesn't work—it catches up with people all too frequently. The case of an employee comes to mind. Almost from the beginning, he was surrounded by rumors of a "checkered past." His boss confronted him with these rumors and invited him to set his record straight. The man denied that there was any truth to the rumors. That was the end of it until a year later, when another person, who had worked with this man before, joined the company. He provided substance to the suspicions, and the man ended up getting fired, and "on the run" for a job. There is a better way to handle your past.

QUESTION

I've been fired from two jobs. I'm not hotheaded or incompetent, and the work that I did was well respected. I simply know my own mind and the direction I want my life and my career to take. I refuse to be manipulated or intimidated into doing something that I'm basically uncomfortable with. I take a stand on my beliefs and accept the consequences.

I now work in a company where very big egos are commonplace. There's an awful lot of backstabbing, and when you look good, there's always somebody there trying to make you look bad. Consequently, I face lots of political hassles.

What scares me is the thought of interviewing for another job. My fear is that a prospective employer will look at my past record and immediately perceive me as a "troublemaker." How can I dispel this image at the start of an interview without causing the interviewer to think that I protest too much?

ANSWER

Frankly, it sounds to me like you are being overly righteous. All relationships, including the one between employee and employer, are the responsibility of both parties. I have the feeling that you don't accept ownership for your part.

The fact is that you have been fired from two jobs. If none of that was your fault, you are at the very least guilty of not having chosen your employers well. Do you *really* know what you want to do? Do you express your desires clearly at your interviews? If you have such strong feelings about the directions you want for your life and career, clarify these before you join a new company, not after.

The best way to minimize the shadow that your prior history casts on your future is to make peace with your own role in it. A prospective employer is more likely to give you another chance if he can see reasons why "this time" it might be different.

THE CONSEQUENCES OF MERGERS ARE UNPREDICTABLE

Of course, many people lose their jobs not because of poor performance but because their company no longer needs them or cannot afford to continue to employ them. While such terminations cause less damage to the individual's career and ego, they impose just as much economic hardship. Furthermore, the fear of losing one's job can be a debilitating factor at the workplace.

QUESTION

I currently work as a sales representative for the local branch of a large organization. Last month we received notice from our parent company that we are going to be sold. What will this bring? What can employees expect in terms of jobs, management, and benefits? We are making money; will that make any difference?

QUESTION

I work for a company that was acquired by a large corporation about two years ago. Since then, we have had two major layoffs. Thus far I've not been affected, but I feel very insecure about my future. My friends have urged me to look elsewhere, but I like my job and feel a sense of loyalty to the company. What do you suggest?

ANSWER

Nobody—not even the management of the acquiring company—can tell in advance precisely what changes an acquisition will bring. The motivation behind an acquisition or a merger is usually to put the resources of the two companies together and, by combining them, accomplish more with the same number of plants, sales offices, and people, or to accomplish the same tasks with fewer plants, etc. In the latter case, layoffs are likely to result.

Generally, the higher you are in the management chain, the more such consolidations are likely to affect you. But even here it is hard to predict exactly how. Your job may be eliminated as the two organizations are combined and streamlined, or you could benefit from new opportunities that your old company would never have been able to offer to you. If the idea behind combining the companies is a good one, it may well be that once the changes are accomplished the new company will be a stronger one, with new avenues for growth for you.

Given the unpredictability of such situations, my suggestion to both of you is to sit tight and watch. There probably will be changes around you for some time (note that in the second writer's situation, they didn't stop even after two years), and while these changes may pose danger to your jobs, they can also bring opportunities.

A PARTNER SLACKS OFF—IS IT THE END?

Something similar to termination can be encountered in the case of partnerships. While one partner usually cannot fire another, the continued existence of a partnership is predicated on all principals pulling their own weight. When that's not the case, the equivalent of termination for cause may be required.

QUESTION

I have a partner with whom I work on a sizable project. I have nothing against partners in principle; in fact, my work requires them. I am concerned, however, with my partner's job performance. His lackadaisical attitude toward our project has caused our employer to question both his *and my* ability to complete the job.

I really resent having my capability questioned because of my partner's lack of motivation. What remedies do you suggest? I have thrown subtle hints but they have had no effect.

ANSWER

This is *no* place for subtle hints! You are talking about your professional reputation and possibly the long-term shape of your career and that's serious business.

Gather your facts and observations, being as specific as possible, and closet yourself with your partner. Your aim should be to leave this meeting with one of three possible outcomes: your partner may have a different perspective on the situation and he convinces you that your evaluation is wrong; or he agrees with your evaluation and firmly rededicates himself to doing a good job; or you conclude that the two of you don't agree.

In the second case, you have to make sure that the commitment is real and is backed up with action. In the course of the discussion, set clear objectives for each of you and agree to review progress jointly. Set up the next review session right then and there.

On the other hand, if the outcome of your discussion is that you can't agree, you have no choice but to break up. My suggestion is that if it comes to this, you pursue the breakup as expeditiously as you can. You shouldn't wait until you both become so resentful and antagonistic that a rational separation becomes impossible.

11

For Better Decisions, Heed Common Courtesy

EMPLOYEES frequently complain about their boss's arbitrariness ("He just went and changed the system without knowing anything about it. Now, nothing works!"). Bosses, in turn, complain about how their employees resist new ideas ("They have closed minds. They won't give anything new a try."). People often say about their bosses, "Unless he thinks it's his idea, he'll fight it tooth and nail." Bosses complain about the endless effort it takes to "sell" their decisions.

MY EMPLOYEES DON'T TAKE ME SERIOUSLY

QUESTION

I have had a management job for five years, but I continue to run into the same problem. Whenever I make a decision, my colleagues don't agree with it and they undermine me and my group. This then makes it even more difficult for me to follow through with my decisions—even the people working for me don't take me seriously.

How can I alleviate this problem?

This writer is one step ahead of most managers in this situation. At least he recognizes that it's up to him to improve matters. Many of his colleagues would be content with merely blaming their coworkers. My answer advocates using a bit of *common courtesy*.

ANSWER

If you have had a problem getting support for your decisions for five years, the problem must be with how you go about trying to implement them. I suspect that you are making decisions without involving your peers and employees. Decisions sprung on others without warning tend to provoke opposition.

Try taking more time in the early stages of your decision-making process. Talk to your colleagues about your pending decision before you make up your mind. Solicit and consider their views.

Discuss various alternatives with them and listen to their reactions. When you have arrived at a definite conclusion, *but before you announce your decision,* visit with them again and tell them what you have decided and why. Then—and only then—make your announcement.

This elaborate process may seem like a waste of time to you at first, but I think you'll find that it will save time in the long run. You'll probably end up with a better decision and one that has support, or at least no opposition, from your coworkers. Such decisions will consequently be easier to implement.

HE SHOT DOWN MY APPROACH!

Take a look at what a very similar situation looks like from the employee's perspective. It illustrates the effect of a sudden edict from above.

QUESTION

I am a college student. I head a committee whose charter is to design and develop a new course. I have spent many hours thinking about how to cope with the large amount of work involved in this task and working around the fact that the other members are also students who are busy with their studies. Eventually I came up with an approach that would divide the work load in a rational fashion, without burying any one of us.

Recently we held a meeting attended by our faculty advisor (our "manager" on this project), in which I presented my approach and divided the work. Our advisor said nothing throughout the meeting until, at the end, I asked him for his opinion. He then shot down my idea totally, in the process demoralizing all of us on the committee. I cannot disregard his objections, particularly since he had some really valid points.

I now have no plan (our advisor didn't propose an alternative approach) and a demoralized group. What did I do wrong and how do I pick up the pieces now?

ANSWER

What you did wrong was not soliciting your advisor's views on this subject earlier. Clearly he must have a lot more experience in developing courses than you do; you should have tapped into this experience *before* your meeting, not during or at the end of it. To judge from his behavior at the meeting, it sounds as if he isn't aggressive in voicing his views. I assume you knew him and his tendencies; all the more reason for you to have taken an earlier initiative to sound him out.

To pick up the pieces, start by picking up your own spirits. You sound crushed and embarrassed by what you view as a defeat. Look at it differently: It was *your approach* that was found wanting, not you. Go back to your advisor and discuss your project with him at greater length. Solicit his ideas—not only on what is wrong with your suggestions but also on better approaches.

Then discuss the new ideas with your fellow committee members with a positive attitude. They are likely to mirror your response to this event: If you view this episode as just a temporary setback that can make your project come out better in the long run, that's how they'll look at it too.

PARTICIPATORY MANAGEMENT: JUST ANOTHER FANCY PHRASE

How much grief could be avoided if everyone at the workplace simply practiced a bit of consideration and courtesy! Current trends in management, including the idea of participatory management, are heading in this direction, even if they often obscure things by making them seem too complex.

QUESTION

I just read an article about participatory management and the problem it causes middle managers. Apparently, this group finds it difficult to accept its new role and feels trapped between the lower and higher levels of management. What can be done to avoid this?

ANSWER

Participatory management is nothing but a fancy phrase that describes the most basic conduct of any competent manager: to solicit ideas and to consult all relevant parties *before* making a decision that affects them. You wouldn't organize a summer picnic at the beach in any other way, that is, without asking the other participants questions like, "What should we bring to eat?" or, "What games should we play?" So, why not approach decisions at work in the same "participatory" way?

I don't think it is the consulting process that causes the pressure. Rather, I believe it stems from the mistaken belief that the process must end with a consensus. It often doesn't, and many managers then feel uncomfortable and under pressure. Participatory management doesn't exempt managers from having to take a stand and make a clear decision *after* everybody has been consulted. That remains part of the job.

As a fledgling supervisor, I felt extremely awkward telling people what to do. In fact, one of my first employees pulled me into his office and gently told me that I really didn't need to apologize each time I gave him direction!

It would certainly be easier and more pleasant if everybody agreed with every decision and a consensus could be reached every time. But if it isn't, a manager must make a decision with or without a consensus. Otherwise, people will go hungry at the picnic.

In the early years of Intel, a major decision, possibly involving the survival of the whole company, faced us. It wasn't for me to make it, but I had strong opinions on the subject. I voiced them in every conceivable forum, over and over. After a period of spirited discussion, the decision was made—I was overruled. I was stumped. I had fully committed myself to the opposite path and now I found myself in an awkward position.

After a day or so of thinking about it, I came to the conclusion that, while I still didn't agree with the choice made by my boss, the only way we could proceed was for me to put all my energy into making his decision work. I did—and it turned out well.

There is an important principle involved here. When a manager makes a decision, it is a must for his employees to *support* it. A decision without the employees' support never has a chance to work. It would be more *pleasant* for all concerned if the employees also *agreed* with the correctness of the decision. Certainly, the boss should put forth a reasonable amount of effort to convince his or her employees of it. But we need to be realistic: Perfectly reasonable people will continue to disagree about many things. They will do so at work too. Yet, for any work to take place at all, once a course has been set, it is a must for all to march in the same direction and to the beat of the same drummer.

So, as boss and employees engage in this touchiest of all work rituals, the decision-making process, they need to keep these simple rules in mind:

• Try to reach agreement on the decision.
• Whether they agree or not, *all* must commit to support the outcome.

NEVER PLAY CHARADES!

Discomfort with one's authority can lead to awkwardness. Even worse, it can cause the manager to act insincerely.

QUESTION

I know that involving one's employees in the decision-making process is beneficial, but is it worth the time when I already know exactly what outcome I want to achieve? Should I go through the steps of participative decision-making, or should I just tell my group what my decision is?

ANSWER

If you truly, truly know what outcome you want and there's no possibility that additional information or insights will change your mind, just go ahead and tell your group what you want. But if you are not 100 percent certain, you should approach them and say, "This is what I think we ought to do. What do you think of it?" Let the group criticize your proposed answer. Its validity will be tested by the ensuing argument.

Under absolutely no circumstances should you play charades and go through an insincere version of a participative decision-making process. This would ruin the integrity of the whole process, and, at another time, when you really want to involve the group, its members will rightly question the seriousness of your approach.

Some managers are seen as dictatorial. Then there are others whom we see as decisive leaders: people who exude and generate confidence in their positions. I have often struggled to figure out the difference between a dictator and a decisive leader. They both seem to be doing the same thing, yet there is a difference.

I think it lies mainly in a sense of appropriateness, or *timing*. For instance, if a manager cuts the deliberation process short and just tells people what the outcome should be, they'll see him as a dictator—and will resist him. If he waits until people have had their say and are themselves ready for a decision to be reached, he will be perceived as an effective leader and his employees will be inclined to follow him.

Of course, if the manager lets the opportunity for a decision pass, and allows the discussion to ramble on without direction, his people will see him as indecisive—which is perhaps the worst alternative.

Let's go back to our picnic example. If the picnic organizer starts out by announcing what everybody will get for lunch, he is almost asking for instant resentment. If he consults the participants for their preferences, scratches his head a bit and then tells what he will bring, providing explanations to those whose choices he could not fulfill, even the latter will accept the outcome with no worse than a shrug. If, on the other hand, he'll take an inordinate amount of time trying to satisfy everybody's taste, valuable picnic time will be lost, and everybody will grow increasingly impatient.

IN AN EMERGENCY, APPLY FIRST AID

Sometimes circumstances require fast action, and the rules of common courtesy must be bypassed.

QUESTION

I work at a small, privately owned company. Recently the owner fired our old boss and hired a new one. The new manager immediately proceeded to change all the operating policies without knowing anything about how things had been done. Is it right for a brand-new manager to assert himself in such a way, or should he make a more gradual transition?

ANSWER

In general, a new, incoming manager should invest some time in getting a feel for how things are done at a place, what works and why, and what doesn't—and why not. Even if he is very sure of how to operate a similar enterprise, those methods and approaches may not work in the new place. Learning, observing, and understanding are keys to figuring out which of his previous methods can be introduced and which shouldn't.

However, there can be exceptions. If your place is in serious trouble (for instance, if it is rapidly running out of cash), the new boss may not have the time to deal with things in a deliberate way. If he has a genuine emergency on his hands, he will have to apply first aid the best way he knows. Drastic and immediate changes may be justified and, in fact, needed, in such cases.

Remember the example of the beach picnic? If you are the first one to notice a strong tide rolling in, it's perfectly appropriate for you to bark orders at your friends, telling them in no uncertain terms to gather their belongings and run for higher ground. Clearly, there are times when seeking consensus can lead to wet blankets or worse.

12

Don't Keep Your Coworkers in the Dark

I have a friend who works at a department store. The store recently installed two-way mirrors and surveillance cameras to guard against shoplifting. I know my friend to be a meticulously honest person, yet he became very upset at this. Nobody had said anything about this change to him or his coworkers, and all immediately assumed that these gadgets were meant to prevent *them* from stealing.

The store management was guilty of a common error: not telling the employees what was going on. This forced them to come up with their own explanation—which was worse than the real story.

This kind of thing frequently happens at the workplace. What's even more troublesome is the worse the news, the stronger the tendency to skirt the issue or to keep quiet about it—even though it's bad news that requires explanation most!

THE COMPANY'S BEEN SOLD—BUT NOBODY TOLD US

QUESTION

I work for a local business that has recently been sold after a year of negotiations. I just read about it in the newspaper. The morale at my office, now that we all know about the sell-off, is unbearably low. What, if anything, should employees be told about conditions that could affect them?

ANSWER

Usually I believe employees should be told as much as possible about the state of the business—both its problems and its opportunities. *If all employees look at the business with similar facts and perspective, they are likely to pull in the same direction,* which is essential in making the business a success.

This is not always possible, however. For instance, negotiations for the sale of your company went on for a year. If management had talked about the deal before it was completed, the sale might have fallen through. Also, your customers might have been scared away by talk of the business being up for sale. In that case, you might not even have a job today. So, in spite of my general leaning toward telling all employees about the state of the business, I can understand why your management did not do so.

But now that the sale of the business is a well-known fact, the morale problems you describe must be dealt with. Your management should get all of you together and walk you through what happened and why. It also needs to share with you its predictions about what the future is likely to bring. All of you need to work hard to clear the air so that you can move forward together.

SHOW YOUR RESPECT BY TELLING IT LIKE IT IS

QUESTION

I am the owner of a small manufacturing firm with twenty-eight employees. The majority are skilled blue-collar workers, many with a union background. Our business environment has become very competitive, and recently I was forced to institute wage and salary cuts and freeze pay levels for the next year.

I am very concerned about the morale of my employees. Can

you give me some suggestions for improving it without adding costs?

ANSWER

Your employees won't be overjoyed with the actions you took no matter what you do. The best you can hope and strive for is that they understand the need for your actions and accept them as reasonable under the circumstances.

To achieve this you must make sure that they fully comprehend the circumstances in which you now find your business. Share your facts with them in as much detail as possible. Let them understand the market conditions you face (who is bidding what, where you lost business and why) and the financial implications for your company (how much money you are making/losing; what your costs are). Then show them how the salary actions you took will help.

This requires a significant effort and time commitment on your part. Do it. You will also feel a strong temptation to paint the situation rosier than it is. Resist that. Keep reminding yourself that you are talking with serious-minded adults from whom you have just required a significant sacrifice. Show your respect to them by telling it like it is!

A MANAGER'S BOMBSHELL BLASTS MORALE TO PIECES

A common bond of knowledge leads to a common outlook, which in turn makes it possible for people to pull together. This principle is often abandoned at precisely the worst of times: We talk freely about good news but are reluctant to share the bad. It's always easy to find reasons why the latter must be kept secret. "Don't demoralize your employees by telling them bad news"—or so the argument goes.

But reality has its own rules, and one is that "bad news always outs," and generally does so in the most demoralizing way.

I learned this when I had to deal with the cancellation of technical projects. Engineers and scientists get terribly devoted to the projects that they work on. When their project gets "killed," whether because of a change in circumstances, lack of results, or because the funding has dried up, they feel betrayed and angry. I found that it helped if I took the time to sit down with the technical people affected by the cancellation and explained to them *why*.

This does not mean that they always bought my arguments. They usually disagreed with them—and me—and said so in no uncertain terms. Still the sense of betrayal and the anger disappeared once they could see how I had come to my conclusion. With a sad sigh, they were then ready to consider their new assignment.

So, the rule is: The worse the news, the more effort should go into communicating it.

QUESTION

I work for an electronics firm. My group's productivity is evaluated by my immediate supervisor, who has always let us believe it was satisfactory. Recently a memorandum by a top executive in our company was posted in our area. It lashed out at us, criticizing our group for low productivity and poor work ethic. It also compared us with a sister plant, claiming that they are better than we are.

We are all upset. Is such comparison a fair thing? Is it right for someone above our immediate supervisor to reveal his displeasure to us?

ANSWER

I see nothing wrong in comparing your group's performance with that of another group. After all, the marketplace compares your company with your competitors daily. Such a comparison, if done objectively and with concrete supporting information, will give you a realistic picture of your own performance and perhaps create a competitive spirit that will make you perform better.

All that is good. However, I am not at all in agreement with the

way this information reached you. It appears that there is a difference of opinion between the top executive and your immediate
supervisor regarding just how well your group performs. This
must be settled between the two of them. In bypassing your boss
and publicly contradicting him, the high-level manager made it
very difficult for your supervisor to do his job, and at the same
time he needlessly upset the entire group. Also, a posted memo is
hardly the way to break bad news to you!

My guess is that there probably *was* a performance problem here,
and that the immediate supervisor was trying to avoid telling his group
bad news. Now, all kinds of energy will be spent in healing the damage caused by this memo—energy that could have been spent more
constructively on improving the group's performance.

RIDE OUT THE WAVE OF BAD NEWS

One should follow the same basic principle in dealing with the
outside world, particularly the press. You may be leery of doing so
when your story isn't wonderful, but, here too, that's when it's most
important.

QUESTION
I work for an organization that has recently been the target of
negative news coverage. How can one limit the extent and the
impact of negative press?

ANSWER
Bad press seems to come in waves. When it hits, there really
isn't much you can do but ride it out. Eventually whatever trig-
gered the rash of negative news coverage will pass and fade.
   Don't try to hide from the press. Your accessibility to them at

such times is more important than ever. Keep in mind that when you talk with the press *you* tell your story. Use the opportunity to try to have them share your perspective of the situation.

THE ONE MOUTH YOU CAN CONTROL IS YOUR OWN

There are some areas that are confidential and that managers should not talk about indiscriminately. One of these is salaries. But even here much can be said without breaking any confidentiality.

QUESTION

I would greatly appreciate some advice on how to handle pay rumors. I am a manager of fifteen production people who tend to discuss with each other what they earn. Consequently, some employees have come to me expressing disappointment after having heard how much John Doe supposedly earns. Sometimes they have it right, other times they are mistaken.

How can I stop such rumors? How do I handle them once they get started?

ANSWER

You'll never stop any rumors, nor can you prevent one employee from talking to another about money matters. The one mouth you can control is your own. Do *not,* ever, discuss with one worker how much another makes; don't confirm someone's salary if your employee has it correctly, and don't correct him if he doesn't. An employee's salary is his or her business and the business of the employer—period.

However, *do* take all the time that is necessary to discuss with each worker how much he or she makes, what raise they got and why, as well as the pay rates that go with their job class and with job classes that may be within their reach. This is their business.

The more information they have, the less impact rumor mills will have.

REACH OUT AND TOUCH YOUR REMOTE
EMPLOYEES—REGULARLY

To achieve good communication at the workplace, you must over-come all kinds of obstacles. We've just dealt with the most difficult one: when we don't *want* to communicate because the news is bad or the subject is awkward. But there are many more—for instance, the difficulty faced by a manager whose people work in distant locations.

QUESTION
I manage four employees who are located in different parts of the United States. All but one have been with the company for less than ten months, and because of travel and budget constraints, they have not been brought to headquarters for training.

What can I do to train, manage, and instill the company's culture in these employees?

ANSWER
Even if you weren't hampered with travel restrictions, having four workers stationed in different locations means that you have to adapt your management approach. Instead of face-to-face meetings, use the telephone. I suggest *regularly scheduled telephone sessions,* at least once a week, with each of them.

Gather all kinds of written material (brochures and articles) about the company and its products and send them to each new employee along with relevant policies and procedures that deal with the "what and how" of their work. Assign portions of this material for study each week. Then, during your scheduled phone calls, discuss the material and how it relates to your employees' daily work.

Supplement these sessions with periodic conference calls where members of your group take turns reporting on their experiences, enabling their peers to learn from them. In addition, ask each of them to write you a weekly report summing up his studies and activities, and encourage them to solicit your help.

Such "long-distance supervision" will be awkward at first, but if you and your group are consistent and disciplined in pursuing it, it will effectively meet your needs.

Such telephone-based communication practices become second nature when you work at a company, like Intel, with offices and plants at many different locations. For example, I find myself routinely involved with regularly scheduled one-on-one meetings conducted on the telephone as well as with large presentations where groups of employees at different locations participate through the use of a telephone hookup. Awkward habits, like gesturing at a squawk box, do take hold—but this approach clearly beats having to travel for hours just to attend a meeting.

A REAL EXPERT CAN TALK IN THE LANGUAGE OF HIS AUDIENCE

All this effort at communicating is for naught, however, if we forget a key rule: How well we communicate is determined not by how well we say things but by how well we are understood. We must have a good measure of our audience—their background, their mood, and their attentiveness. While we can't change any of these, as communicators we *can* and *must* tailor our message so it's appropriate.

I gave a talk some years ago. My hosts had painted a picture of a highly sophisticated and knowledgeable audience, so I prepared a complex and highfalutin talk. Ten minutes into my presentation, the blank eyes staring at me told me something was wrong. I stopped and asked the audience if they followed me. After some hesitancy, a few people started to shake their heads, no. Some more questions established the real background of my audience, which was far less expert than what I was led to believe.

I put away my prepared notes and launched into an informal and elementary discussion on my appointed subject. This the audience followed; my evening turned out to be successful, after all, even if most of my preparation was left unused.

QUESTION

I work for a management consultant who has asked me to give a presentation to clients based on material that he had prepared. Subsequently he criticized me for using layman's terms, saying that those are not appropriate in business. Do you agree?

ANSWER

Not at all! Using complex terms, in my view, is a symptom of one of two things. Either the person using them intends to make himself sound more knowledgeable and sophisticated than he is, or he is too lazy to work on removing language that may have become professional jargon but has no meaning to outsiders.

Either reason is wrong. The more knowledgeable any one of us is in a given field, the more we should be able to explain our thoughts in the language of our audience. In fact, I tend to view the simplicity by which an expert expresses himself as an indication of both the depth of his knowledge and his self-confidence. So, stick to your guns and work on making yourself understood by your clients.

DON'T PERMIT SHYNESS TO STIFLE YOU

QUESTION

I am basically a shy person and have difficulty speaking up at meetings. By the time I force myself to participate, the discussion has moved on to the next subject. I do good work and accomplish a lot, but it's done in my own quiet way, outside of these meetings. I feel that my chances for further advancement are limited because of my shyness. Is that right? Is there something I can do about it?

ANSWER

Even if you do good work, the shyness that you describe deprives your employees, your coworkers, and your boss—and therefore your company—from something valuable. Even diligent and efficient work behind the scenes can't substitute for not contributing to an issue while it's being considered and debated. The right time for making comments is while everybody's attention is focused on the subject.

You can't change your personality, but you can force yourself to participate in group discussions. Remind yourself that your opinions are more valuable when they are timely. Work on making yourself speak up at meetings. Maybe you can begin by supporting the statements of others with whom you agree. Keep talking even if at first your comments are not as sage as you'd like them to be. I think you will eventually get the hang of it.

ON THE JOB, THERE'S ROOM FOR ONLY ONE LANGUAGE

I started this chapter by pointing out that knowledge held in common is what makes it possible for people to pull together. It is fitting, then, to end it with some exchanges that underscore the point in yet another fashion.

QUESTION

I am a recent immigrant to the United States. I work for a medium-sized electronics company that has a policy of not allowing the use of a foreign language at work. Is that right?

ANSWER

The policy is a good one. Nothing will separate people at work into little cliques more rapidly than the use of a language others don't understand, and such cliques can only hurt the productivity of the company. The only common language in the U.S. *is* English. Speaking English at work is crucial.

QUESTION

I work for a foreign-based firm. Most of the other employees are Chinese, and they generally speak Chinese except when speaking to me or to clients. When I accepted the job, I did not realize how depressing this situation could be.

Even worse, because the language isolates me so much, I find it very difficult to figure out what the firm's policy is or what its attitude is toward certain matters. For example, one of my colleagues deals with clients in a way that I consider very unprofessional, yet I can't tell whether or not our director approves of such behavior. I want to leave, yet I feel doing so would be cowardly. What do you advise?

ANSWER

Your situation sounds awful. By being surrounded by a language you don't understand, you are deprived of the daily interaction and give-and-take that make work rewarding and which are necessary for your own development. You must change the situation, one way or another.

Your coworkers and your boss simply may not realize what impact their use of their native language has on you. I suggest that you first sit down with your boss and explain it to him—exactly as you have in your letter. Keep the discussion focused on what this situation does to you and how it isolates you from your boss and your coworkers.

I must admit that I am doubtful that your boss will have the determination to make a consistent change in a habit as ingrained as the use of his native tongue, but you must give it a try just so you won't feel later that you ran away from a situation without attempting to change it.

Set a time limit—say, two or three weeks—and see if a change is forthcoming. When the time period is up and there is no change, look for another job with dispatch. Your own career development is at stake.

A READER'S RESPONSE

I read your answer to the person who works for a predominantly Chinese-speaking firm. It really bothers me. Why do you recommend that the whole company change to meet his needs? Is it entirely out of the question that he make an effort to learn to speak Chinese? It seems to me that the employee should be willing to meet his bosses halfway, especially since, in this case at least, he is in the minority. Must we Americans always insist that our language is the only "right" one?

ANSWER

As an immigrant myself, I have strong feelings on this subject. This country "works" because of the diversity of people who have come here from all corners of the world and because all these people have learned to live and work with each other as one nation. That means that we must have one language, which happens to be English. The obligation to adjust is with the newcomers.

Aside from the principles involved, think of the practicality of your suggestion: Would you expect employees to learn a new language each time they change jobs? Incidentally, the person who wrote the original question has written to me again; she has given up and decided to leave her job. This solves her problem, but her replacement will face the same difficulty.

13

I Don't Have Time!

NOTHING about our work seems to get us as panicky as the feeling that we are running out of time to do all of what we think we must do. As the sense of panic grips us, we start slashing about in the time-management equivalent of hyperventilation. We then do an increasingly poor job of coping with the tasks at hand.

QUESTION

I run a small business. I find that no matter how many hours I work, I can't fit all the things I need to do into my working day. Any suggestions?

QUESTION

I manage a department whose responsibilities have grown more rapidly than its staffing. We all have to bust a gut just to get the product out the door. As a result, most of us spend much of our time fighting brushfires. We have no time for planning, and we don't accomplish as much as we might.

Increased staffing without even more work seems out of the question. What can we do to improve the situation?

ANSWER

Your problem is very common. We always seem to have more work than we are staffed for. Our response then follows an equally common pattern: We try to do all that is expected, more or less at the same time. Even as we work harder and harder, we fall "behinder and behinder," as the saying goes.

Next, as we start taking shortcuts to speed things up, the quality of our work begins to suffer, and we find ourselves having to redo things, further compounding our work load.

Even if at this point, to avert a catastrophe, we get permission to hire more staff, we clearly won't have time to interview candidates properly, or to train them once they're hired. And so it goes . . .

To break this self-destructive chain, assess how much you are capable of doing and fight off all temptation (and pressure) to do more. Put the things you must do in order of importance and start at the top of the list. When you are done with the first project, review those remaining, put them in order again (your sense of priorities may have changed) and go to work on the top one again. Prioritizing your projects and concentrating on the top one will take self-discipline and courage, but *there is no other way*.

You wouldn't speed up boarding a bus by squeezing passengers through the door three at a time. In the same way you won't accomplish much by trying to do more work than you and your staff are capable of.

While selectivity is a must, I admit that it's much easier to prescribe than to practice. I get a reminder every time I go on a longer business trip. My departure is a firm deadline for all of my activities at the office—the plane leaves whether everything I need to do is completed or not. This non-negotiable deadline, coupled with the need to clean up all pending matters that I would otherwise deal with during the time I am on the trip, invariably puts a great deal of extra pressure on me.

During such times I am forced to practice the selectivity I just preached to the utmost. My adrenalin usually starts pumping about a week before my last day at the office. From then on, I survey my work load with a ruthlessness that stems from my desire to survive: I only get involved with meetings, issues, calls, or visitors that meet some unwritten but very stringent set of criteria; everything else I firmly defer to someone else. *(Delaying* requests for my time won't work at such times, as I know from experience that the period after my return will also be a very hectic one.)

The principles that guide me are not to get involved in anything that I can't finish and to dispose (by referring the task to someone else or simply by saying no) of all other matters. If I succeed, I board my plane exhausted but with no dangling matters left behind.

Selectivity—the determination to choose what we will attempt to get done and what we won't—is the only way out of the panic that excessive demands on our time can create.

There is no miracle drug for the next writer's problem either.

THE SOLUTION IS TO BE DOUBLY RIGOROUS

QUESTION

I recently was moved into a new position and I am sinking. My desk is buried under paper that I can't handle fast enough because everything is still unfamiliar. My people have a hard time getting my attention. I forget things, and I never used to do that in my prior job. I've tried every time-management technique I know, but nothing seems to make any difference. I feel like a loser. What can I do to get on top of my work again?

ANSWER

First, don't be too hard on yourself. When you are new at a job, everything takes longer because you are not familiar with procedures and history. It's almost as if you had become slower and dumber from one day to the next. Time on the job will help take care of that.

Meanwhile, become even more meticulously organized than you used to be. Don't allow papers to bury your desk, and make an extra effort to block out time for your new employees. Be *doubly rigorous* in organizing your time: Plan your activities at the start of each day, set priorities for yourself, schedule desk time, and—most importantly—write everything down so nothing can fall through the cracks.

Let me warn you about the most common pitfall in this situation. As these measures start doing some good and as you achieve some control over your paperwork, your information, and your time, you'll be tempted to relax and become less rigorous again in sticking to your time-management practices. Fight off this temptation, or else you'll have to go through this terrible phase again and again. The techniques are simple; what makes them magical is sticking with them consistently!

CHANNEL INTERRUPTIONS INTO A REGULAR PATTERN

I know of only two basic ways by which a person can improve his use of time: One is better selectivity, as we've just discussed; the other is introducing as much *regularity* into one's daily work as possible. Search for a pattern in what you need to accomplish and use that pattern to your advantage. Group similar activities together instead of jumping from one to the other. For instance, gather all your pending phone calls and sit down to make them one after the other. In case you don't reach people, set aside a time slot and request a callback during that time.

Unfortunately, introducing and maintaining regularity in your schedule requires more of that elusive self-discipline. Having tried both, I'll opt for self-discipline over "gasping for time" any day.

QUESTION

When I was a beginning manager, I decided that I'd always have an open-door policy. I've continued that policy through the years, and employees seem to like it. There's only one problem: My paperwork is piling up. What do you suggest?

ANSWER

Your open-door policy is a good one, not only because your employees like it, but also because it demonstrates that dealing with the issues they bring to your attention is a major part of your job.

The trick is to channel your interaction with your people into a regular, scheduled form so you can maintain the rest of your time for other matters, like your paperwork.

Establish regularly scheduled meetings with the people who tend to come barging in with questions and concerns. This way you can direct your dealing with their problems into a time slot set aside for that purpose. These meetings will not eliminate interruptions, but they'll certainly help to reduce them. If your employees know that they have a meeting coming up with you next Tuesday at ten A.M., they'll often decide to hold their questions until then.

An office hour is another alternative. Simply hang a sign on your door that says, "I am doing individual work. Please don't interrupt me until two P.M. unless it really can't wait." Then at two P.M., open your door and be receptive to anybody who wants to see you.

Accessibility reaches its ultimate form when the work environment is an "open office": individual work areas separated by low partitions over which you can see standing up. There are *no* doors in such an arrangement, and people can even talk to you over the top of the partition, although this is considered to be bad form.

This arrangement makes it easier for your employees to approach you with their problems. Look at that not as a burden but as an opportunity to get early warning of trouble that would catch up with you sooner or later anyway.

In one instance, as I stood up in my office, I noticed over my partition that an employee who was visiting from an overseas location was hanging around my office. I had a feeling that he wanted to talk to me. So, I said hello to him. He eagerly came over and after a few minutes started telling me about a major problem that was developing at his branch location, and which he felt was not being taken seriously enough at the home office. His warning gave me the opportunity to go to work on this situation perhaps months before I might have otherwise—and helped avert a much bigger problem. This short interruption saved our company from a lot of trouble—and saved me a whole lot of time!

CREATE HOLES TO CATCH YOUR BREATH AFTER MEETINGS

Next to interruptions, *meetings* are seen as the biggest time sink at the workplace.

QUESTION

I manage a department in a municipal government organization. My problem is that my schedule is crammed with meetings that I am required to attend. As I go from one to another, I tend to forget things I was asked to do in the course of the day. When I realize I dropped a ball, I get tense and can't even pay attention to what's being said, which makes my problem even worse. What can I do to break this chain?

ANSWER

You *must* create holes in your schedule in which you can catch your breath! They may be very brief but they should take place after each meeting, without fail. Sit down at your desk or in the corner of a meeting room and reflect for a few minutes on the meeting that just ended. Take a piece of paper and jot down what you need to do as a result of that meeting—like, whom you need to call or what information you must supply to someone. Write down these tasks in clear, complete sentences so you'll be able to follow your own notes even after another meeting has shifted your attention elsewhere.

This practice may not create time for you—only getting out of some of those "obligatory" meetings will do that—but it will help maintain your sanity and effectiveness.

A SECRETARY NEEDS A BOSS'S TIME

A manager who is fortunate enough to have a secretary is way ahead in his or her struggle with time. A secretary can help not only by relieving the manager of certain tasks, but also by helping him maintain self-discipline instead of succumbing to panic. But before a secretary can do that, the manager must do much coaching and teaching. And—here is the catch—this, at first, is another time drain.

QUESTION
I was just assigned a secretary. I've never had one before and would like to start the right way. How can I train my secretary to help me most?

ANSWER
Invest your most precious resource, your time, and train your secretary systematically. Focus the training specifically on the contents of your job. If your secretary understands *what* you do and *why*, he or she will do things in a way that's consistent with how you would do them yourself.

Take the routine tasks of your office, such as setting up meetings or handling your incoming phone calls, and walk through them. Ask your secretary to keep a record of what you have covered; this will create a handy reference for later use. Arrange to have him or her meet some of the individuals with whom you have frequent contact—a fifteen-minute meeting conducted without pressing matters hanging over the participants will build a good foundation for future dealings.

Don't stop with just a basic familiarization. Set up weekly one-on-one meetings with your secretary in which you spend half an hour reviewing the events of the past week and those of the upcoming week. These sessions will fine-tune your secretary's knowledge of the job and enable him or her to help you more and more. *Investing time in your secretary may be the best investment you ever make.* It will be repaid with dividends, in the form of time saved.

TOO MUCH OF A GOOD THING—
AT WORK, TOO

While you are concerned with your own time problems, keep an eye out for your employees, too. One major way you can assist their development is to guide them in solving their time problems. Chances are that you are more experienced at coping with the pressures of the workplace, so share what you have learned. As their boss, you also control the work load, giving you additional ways to help your employees stay afloat.

QUESTION

I have a problem that I suppose many managers would like to have. One of my employees works too hard—and I mean much too hard. She insists on handling everything herself and refuses to delegate anything.

She maintains that she "wants it done right." I can't disagree with the fact that she does good work, but she's spending fourteen to sixteen hours a day at the office, and the strain is beginning to show. She's become tense and snappy, and I fear she is hurting morale. I'm also beginning to have real concerns for her health. Telling her to go home doesn't work. How do I slow her down without discouraging her or taking away her enthusiasm?

ANSWER

You're right to be concerned. The person you describe is probably on a long-term downward spiral. If nothing is done, she could damage herself and diminish her usefulness to the company. So, helping her isn't just the decent thing to do, it's also good for the business.

Start by describing your observations to her in a rational, objective manner. Try to convince her that she must slow down and delegate some of her activities. She will probably argue that she must do all these things because nobody else is there to do them. Point out that if she gets seriously ill, everything would end up undone.

Offer to lighten her assigned work load. Discuss ways her job can be divided. I suspect she won't like that solution, but it might give her the needed push to streamline what she does and fit it into a reasonable workday. But if this doesn't happen, follow through and lighten her work load yourself.

Bear in mind that just as some paranoids may truly be persecuted, some workaholics might in fact be carrying too heavy a work load. If this is the case, it's your responsibility to correct the situation.

WRITE NOTES TO YOURSELF—
SO YOU WON'T FORGET

As a famous mountain climber once said, a climber doesn't conquer mountains, he conquers himself. So it is with controlling one's time: With all the good advice in the world, managing your time consists of managing yourself. And each of us has different capabilities and weaknesses. Understanding what they are is the first step to being able to conquer our own "time mountain."

QUESTION

I have a problem I'm almost too embarrassed to bring up. I forget things. I attend meetings in which I am given assignments that I fully intend to undertake, but then I get distracted and forget about the assignment until it's too late. My forgetfulness has already caused me considerable problems with my managers and my colleagues, and seems likely to limit my performance in the future unless I find a solution.

I have tried various methods like carrying notebooks and other reminders around with me, but they don't help because I lose track of them and never have them handy when I need them. Also, many of my ideas come to me as I am walking around the laboratory, and I certainly am not carrying my reminder book with me there. Any suggestions?

ANSWER

The simplest solution is the best. Whenever you need to, write yourself a one- or two-word note on *anything* you have available—a piece of paper, the margin of a newspaper, or a matchbook cover.

When you get back to your office, immediately take out your

pieces of paper and write yourself a more intelligible, complete reminder in a notebook that you *always keep in your office.* Review this notebook several times a day and cross out those assignments that you have completed.

The key is that the notebook should always stay in one place, rather than travel around with you. The constant practice of transferring brief notes into your notebook should create a habit that will benefit you in two ways: You will continually refer to your notebook, and the practice of writing yourself reminders twice will fix them in your memory.

INSTANT ACTION CAN CURE PROCRASTINATION

QUESTION

Please excuse me for writing this in such a sloppy way, but I am afraid of postponing writing to you altogether. So, I am writing to you from a coffee shop, just having finished reading your column.

I am a highly educated, reasonably bright person, a really hard worker. My problem is, whenever a task is assigned to me or I get an idea about something, I immediately postpone doing something about it. I somehow tell myself I have more important things to do now and keep putting the action off until the last moment. Then, when I finally do what I need to do, I find it really easy and usually it doesn't even take much time.

I end up saying to myself, "I should have done this a long time ago . . ." What can I do to change this terrible habit?

ANSWER

Do exactly what you did in this instance—do something right after the task is given to you or when an idea strikes you.

Take some immediate action, even if you'll be going off half-cocked.

Such instant action may break the spell of procrastination. You may have to refine your work later, but having started the task, you'll find it easier to return to it promptly.

14

The Mating Game: Employer Meets Employee

THE game of corporate mating—the process through which companies and future employees meet, evaluate each other, and make their selection—is not a very efficient one. I'd say it's a bit more systematic than the way people find their romantic mates but not nearly as well organized as the real estate marketplace, which matches up people with houses.

For one thing, neither job applicants nor companies have a very clear picture of what they are looking for. Sure, the applicant's résumé contains the obligatory paragraph describing the position desired, and the company has a description on file of the ideal candidate; but neither party can really put into words what the ideal job or candidate would look like.

A friend of mine solicited my advice about how to find a job in the industrial world. She is a sophisticated woman, a teacher, who decided that she wanted to try working in industry. Having a pretty good idea of what types of jobs there are, I tried to ask her, "What about this—and what about that?" We didn't get very far—none of the positions I named meant anything to her.

Eventually she responded to an ad for a position as inventory-control supervisor. She had little idea of what this position was about and was quite frightened by the obscure and seemingly complex requirements that were listed in the ad. Neither did her interviewer feel comfortable about considering a schoolteacher for this job. The interview got off to an awkward start, with both applicant and interviewer feeling their way along. But slowly they established a common language and began getting acquainted. My friend got the job and after a period of training did well with it.

One of the difficulties is the limited time and exposure the prospective employer and employee have available. How can either party make a truly sound selection on the basis of one or two brief interviews?

LEARN ABOUT PAST PERFORMANCE AND SEE IF YOU CAN COMMUNICATE WITH EACH OTHER

QUESTION

My problem involves determining the right things to look for in a job applicant. Some of my peers have hired several excellent people for positions within their departments. Unfortunately, I've hired a couple of losers, and I don't want to keep making the same mistake.

Are there certain questions to ask potential employees that would help me make better judgments?

ANSWER

Don't look for magic solutions. Selecting a candidate for a job is one of the most nebulous activities a manager performs. Focus the selection process on establishing only two things: the performance record of the candidate and your ability to communicate effectively with him or her.

The interview itself should be looked upon as only a part of the selection process; it should be supplemented by checking with references who can give an independent assessment of the applicant's past performance: What did the candidate do in his previous jobs? How well did he do it? But to get this information from a reference, you must ask pertinent and relevant questions. One purpose of the interview is to give you enough background to be able to do that.

Use your questioning to discover exactly what your candidate has done in his previous positions. Ask him to describe his earlier activities in as much detail as you can understand. Have him elaborate on what he liked and disliked, and on what he considers his biggest accomplishment, as well as his biggest failure. In short, have the candidate talk about his past work.

Also, use the interview to determine your ability to communicate by finding out how well the candidate understands you and how he responds to your questions. For instance, does the candidate provide only superficial answers to your questions? Or does he or she overwhelm you with detail?

This will take time. In fact, you should probably interview the candidate more than once and have your own assessments validated by your boss and associates through additional interviews. There's just no shortcut for all this. The task is very difficult, and the consequences of hiring the wrong person are serious.

And the worst of it is, even when you do your homework and do it thoroughly, the results are by no means guaranteed. A painful example comes to mind in which I took particular pains to find the right person for a critical job. I did everything, absolutely everything, that I advise above. The highly favorable impressions I gained through my two long and thorough interviews were reinforced by the applicant's record and, most importantly, by the comments of several people who had worked with him in his prior jobs.

We hired the person, and he was disappointing from the very beginning. Sometime later, when I stopped rationalizing and accepted that I had made a terrible mistake (not my first of this kind and, as it turns out, not my last), we parted company. When I ran into one of the individuals who had served as a reference and told him of the outcome, he said he wasn't really surprised. I questioned him, and he told me that the problems I had with this man were the same he had with him in prior years. "Why didn't you tell me?" I asked, filled with a mixture of frustration and anger. He answered, "I didn't want to be in his way. I thought he had learned his lesson when I fired him."

PRESENT YOURSELF AS YOU ARE

During an interview, both applicant and interviewer are on display and often aim to present themselves in a way that makes them attractive to the other party. It's OK to help insure that the other party notices your good features. But it is of no use to feign characteristics that are not true. A good impression based on pretense is not likely to last.

QUESTION
What skills or qualifications do you feel are important when an employer is looking at a prospective employee who is fresh out of college?

ANSWER
Most of us look for young people who are eager to do something with what they've learned in college—whatever their field might be. We look for people who like working and producing in school because they are likely to be equally productive at work.

We look for energy, openness, a readiness to learn—there is so much more to learn once you start working. But no matter what *we* are looking for—at all costs, be yourself. Attempting to present yourself as something other than what you really are will backfire. You will either not be chosen, or you will get a job that doesn't suit you. Then you are likely to be unhappy, and unhappy workers usually don't succeed.

YOU SHOULD WARN AN INTERVIEWER GENTLY ABOUT ILLEGAL QUESTIONS

Today's interviewer is constrained by a variety of laws keeping him from asking questions about such things as the applicant's age and marital status. Not too surprisingly, not all follow these restrictions rigorously, posing some interesting problems for the applicant.

QUESTION
What should I do when I'm in an interview and the interviewer asks illegal questions like, "Are you married?" or, "How many children do you plan to have?"

If I don't answer the questions, I won't get the job, but by answering them I sanction the interviewer's behavior.

ANSWER
Keep in mind that most interviewers probably aren't even aware of the fact that some of their questions are potentially discriminatory; even if they've been trained in the law, it's easily forgotten.

Answer the first such question that's asked. Then add a gentle comment like, "I thought questions of this kind are no longer permitted." You might even phrase it in the form of a question: "Aren't questions relating to marital status forbidden?" I expect most interviewers will be taken back by such a reminder and be much more cautious after that; yet, by being inoffensive you will avoid antagonizing them.

IMMIGRANTS FACE EXTRA HURDLE IN JOB MARKET

The United States is perhaps the most open society in the world toward immigrants. Even so, credentials earned in another country are hard to import. If a prospective employer is not familiar with the educational system or business practices of an applicant's country of origin, he is likely to downgrade experience acquired there.

When an immigrant has additional handicaps, his disadvantage is greatly compounded. It takes a great deal of perseverance—and a willingness to compromise—to overcome such obstacles.

QUESTION

At the age of twenty-one I was the youngest purchasing manager of a large Hong Kong electronics company. By the age of twenty-seven, I was considered a very successful businessman in my country. I decided that I could move to the United States and become even more successful.

But it's been six months, and I haven't even gotten a job interview. I went from applying for high-income jobs to looking for what I consider to be very medium-income jobs. I can't figure out if I'm being discriminated against for my age or nationality or if I'm considered to be unskilled because I don't have a degree.

I've sent résumés to countless companies, and all I get are "thanks, but no thanks," replies. Should I hang on or pack up and go home?

ANSWER

You face a problem common to all immigrants. It's never easy to bring one's qualifications and experience into another country and have them accepted at face value. Because we all tend to evaluate an individual's accomplishments in a familiar framework, immigrants face an additional difficulty in a new country where the schools they attended and the firms they worked for are unknown. While it may be unfair, achievements made in a foreign country tend to be discounted.

If you want to build a life and career in the United States, accept this and lower your initial expectations. Look for a starting position for which you are clearly *over*qualified. Then, even if your experience in your home country is a bit ambiguous and difficult to evaluate, your employer won't feel that he's taking a big chance with you. If you are as good as you say you are, your contributions will be recognized, and you'll be promoted rapidly.

QUESTION

I am a Vietnamese and disabled—I lost a leg in the war. I graduated as an electrical engineer nine months ago. I am very interested in working in electronics but I am very frustrated: I cannot get a job. I wonder if it's because of prejudice against me as a foreigner. What should I do?

ANSWER

While being an immigrant carries its special difficulties, I think being disabled burdens you with an even more difficult handicap. With so many graduates looking for jobs, it's easy for an employer to turn to another candidate. But whether this is prejudice or something else matters little. The fact is that you face more difficulties than other new job applicants.

Try to find other physically disabled individuals who have succeeded in finding jobs; they can give you some much-needed support. It also may be that you'll have to compromise and accept a job that is below your qualification, where you represent— please forgive the expression—a "bargain." Ideally, you shouldn't have to do this but, realistically, it may be necessary for you to get a start.

Once you are in and you can be evaluated by what you *do* and not what you are, I believe that neither your physical disability nor being foreign-born will keep you from advancing.

DON'T UNDERESTIMATE YOUR YEARS AS MOTHER AND HOUSEWIFE

Another whole group of candidates for employment suffers from difficulties similar to those encountered by immigrants—even if they've spent their entire lives in this country. They are the women who attempt to reenter working life after years of absence.

QUESTION

I am a mother of three children and have been out of the workplace for a number of years. I was a secretary before I started raising my family. Now that my children are all in school, I want to go back to work.

I have two concerns. I'm afraid that while I was away from the business world many things have changed there. So, I'm not sure if I still have the right qualifications for the type of work I used to do. Also, I don't know what to put on my résumé to convince an employer that I'd be a good candidate for employment.

ANSWER

You are right; things *have* changed in the office in the last several years. You definitely need to learn a number of new skills that are commonplace in today's offices, *in addition* to boning up on the skills you used to have but probably did not use during the years you were home. I suggest you enroll immediately in a number of courses—partly to acquire such skills but also to re-build your self-confidence. Most junior colleges offer them.

Regarding your résumé—don't underestimate your years as a mother and housewife. Consider them as a period of time in which you performed a very difficult task—raising a family of three children. As you must know better than I do, in that time you learned to manage your time (often under highly conflicting demands), set priorities, make decisions (frequently under immense pressure), anticipate difficulties, and solve problems (usually more than one at a time). This experience increased your maturity and honed your common sense.

Combined with a refreshed set of skills, your personal development during these child-rearing years should make you a valuable candidate for reentry into the business world.

This is how *you* should look at it, and this is also how you should portray it in your résumé and in job interviews.

GET A FEEL FOR YOUR FUTURE WORK AND WORK AREA

We have been talking about getting a foot in the door. But it's important that the employee should get his or her foot in the *right* door! In the course of the job search and interview process, the applicant also needs to evaluate the employer: the boss, the department, and the company.

The future employer should encourage this evaluation. His hiring and training investment will be wasted if the employee quits because he finds that he's made a poor choice.

An engineer I know went to work for a company as a designer. The people at this company who interviewed her built up the job as a very exciting and stimulating one, appealing to her desire for technical challenge. When she started work, she was put through an extensive training program in the computerized design methods used at this firm. Eventually, she was ready to start designing. To her dismay, she found that design work at this company was systematized and computerized to such a degree that it consisted of little more than pushing buttons in a predetermined sequence. Disappointed, she quit a few months later—her and the firm's investment both went to waste.

QUESTION

When I look for a new job, I like to take into account the atmosphere in the area where I'll be working. I can usually establish the general characteristics of a company by reading about it and talking with people outside of the company. However, I don't know how to go about forming an accurate impression of the work environment. What can you suggest?

ANSWER

The best way is through people who work in that group. Ask them to talk about what it's like to work there. A few anecdotes would probably paint a pretty clear picture.

In the course of your interview, ask to see your future work area. Walk around and keep your eyes open. Look at the layout, the pace, the dress style, the decor. Ask your escort about minor things like where people eat lunch and where they go during their breaks. Find out if members of the group socialize outside of work.

Trust your intuition: Even ten minutes spent in the work area looking around and listening to the answers to such random questions will give you a good sense of the place.

BE WARY OF A COMPANY THAT HIRES INDISCRIMINATELY

Here is a case where the applicant's sense provided an early warning of the true nature of the workplace.

QUESTION

I started a new job this year, and in just a few months I have seen a tremendous turnover in my department. I have to conclude that the reason for this is poor management.

I became suspicious when I got the job without filling out an application or giving my boss a résumé. Once I was hired, he never defined my job objectives. No one else in the department has had their objectives defined either. I believe this kind of disorganization causes a great deal of dissatisfaction among the employees. I have gotten to where I hate the place!

Is this common practice for a large company? What should I do about it?

ANSWER

The practices you describe are not at all common, and they are *terrible* for either large or small companies. I don't think you should invest your time in a company that hires you without getting basic information on your background.

Run, don't walk, to the exit, just as many of your coworkers have, and look for a job in a better environment. Only a place with decent management practices is capable of rewarding your performance and aiding your development.

Career development is an incredibly random process. A young person is exposed to only a small sampling of possible careers, mostly the occupations of parents, relatives, and family friends. I feel strongly that young people should be encouraged to "get their hands dirty" and gain early work experience. If nothing else, this will remove some of the haze through which they inevitably view their possible choices of work.

Summer jobs are particularly useful in this regard: They enable a student to experiment. The varied experiences I gained through my half dozen or so summer jobs have definitely helped guide the direction of my education and have provided me with practical experience that serves me well to this day.

In one I worked twelve-hour shifts of backbreaking labor; in another I worked in a plant that had no regard for safety—and I saw its consequences firsthand (my friend was severely burned in a totally preventable fire); elsewhere I found out what office politics are like when carried to the extreme: I watched a set ritual in which all members of a department showed up at work on Saturday and would then shoot the breeze until the big boss left. Shortly after that, their immediate supervisor would depart, and minutes later everybody else was heading home. What a waste of a good Saturday morning!

At the same time these jobs gave me a chance to practice what I had learned in school. This helped me find out more specifically what it was that I liked to do and what I was good at. There is nothing like real-life experience to guide a person's career development.

FOR A CAREER IN MARKETING, FIRST LEARN TO *SELL*

QUESTION

I am a business student, majoring in marketing. I have heard a lot of encouraging comments about what a good field marketing is, especially for women, but I am also hearing comments about the need for hands-on experience. Is it really necessary? What kind of experience would be most useful?

ANSWER

Marketing work is very closely related to the act of *selling*. In fact, that's the reason for its existence. So I think it would be extremely useful for you to work in *sales*—of any kind. There's a lot in the sales process that's independent of the goods and services being sold, and much of it you can only learn through experience.

I strongly recommend that you look for work in sales, either while you are studying marketing or before you start working in it. It doesn't have to involve sophisticated products or be in the field you ultimately want to work in—but it should expose you to the experience of dealing with customers face-to-face and making sales.

Experience the process, its joys and its disappointments; experience firsthand what helps and hinders the closing of a sale, and it will help you throughout your marketing career.

CLASSROOM KNOWLEDGE CAN'T REPLACE REAL-LIFE EXPERIENCE

QUESTION

I'm a business major. I thoroughly enjoy reading about business and I am wondering if it would be possible for me to learn enough about business strategies, practices, and history to put this knowledge to use at a high-level position when I graduate?

ANSWER

Will it be possible for you to get a high-level job when you graduate? Undoubtedly. Many business graduates do, every year. Will you be qualified for such a job? Not in my view.

Book or classroom learning, useful as it is in building an intellectual foundation, is limited in how well it can prepare a person for a real-life job. It cannot reproduce the emotional setting in which business activities are performed, decisions are made, contracts are negotiated, and people problems are dealt with. There is simply no substitute for experience.

It's a bit like trying to learn tennis from a book. You may learn every stroke by studying pictures and memorize every game strategy, but would you ever win a tournament that way?

15

Advancement Ambitions/ Promotion Pitfalls

PROMOTIONS—increased job responsibility, advancement up the rungs of the career ladder—are very important. To an individual they are the most tangible and valuable reward for performance on the job. They are also important to the manager who makes the selection: A well-chosen promotion will contribute greatly to his or her future success on the job. And, of course, they matter greatly to other workers who considered themselves candidates.

Therefore, it's imperative that managers do the best job they can in selecting the right people for higher-level jobs. The selection should be based on past performance—and little else—partly because past performance is the only reliable basis from which future performance can be predicted and also because a promotion represents a highly visible statement of what is really valued by management.

BASE CHOICE ON PERFORMANCE—NOT ON PERSONALITY

QUESTION

I am a section head responsible for about twenty people at a large engineering corporation. I've just been promoted, but before I can assume my new responsibilities, I have to recommend a replacement for myself.

I have two candidates who are total opposites. I believe both could be successful in my job. Candidate #1 is conservative, diligent, extremely hardworking, and handles himself well, although he is quiet and reserved. He pays attention to every detail, which is important on this job. Candidate #2 is aggressive, dynamic, and open, but is neither as consistent nor as precise as candidate #1. However, he is a terrific motivator of people.

Which one should I choose?

ANSWER

Your descriptions of the two candidates characterize them vividly, but they don't really provide a basis for choice. No single set of characteristics makes for a good manager. Different individuals bring different sets of skills and attributes to their work. Some combinations work well and other very similar combinations don't—consequently, there's no way of making a distinction that is always valid.

Go back and study the past performance of these two individuals. Have they been tested in a variety of jobs and environments? What did they accomplish in their prior assignments? Don't dwell on their personalities. Concentrate on the *results* they produced. Choose the individual with the best performance record.

This is such an obvious point—yet we have so much difficulty following it! It's as if we were infected with the proverbial central-casting mentality. All too often our first inclination is to choose somebody who *looks* the part. If we are lucky, we stop ourselves before we act on this urge and let the individual's past performance be the determinant. If we aren't so lucky, we choose the person whose looks and characteristics seem to fit—then we spend the next year or so reluctantly coming to terms with our error.

Some years ago I had to choose a production manager. There were a number of candidates for the position. Having had a research background, I had a hard time telling one production executive's background from another's. So I chose the individual who most closely approximated my idea of what a production manager should be like. He was personable, dynamic, outspoken—a real go-getter. He turned out to be quite ineffective in the job. As I found out later, after more digging, he had not been very effective in his prior assignments either. His successor was a quiet man, thoughtful, a bit slow-moving, but whatever he touched worked and continued to work. I learned a lesson—the hard way.

The handling of promotions has an enormous potential for bringing office politics, game playing, and deviousness into the workings of an organization. To minimize this the promotion process should be handled in the most objective, open, and straightforward fashion possible—by all parties.

INSTEAD OF VYING FOR ATTENTION, CONCENTRATE ON YOUR JOB

QUESTION

I work for a specialty store. Our department recently lost its assistant manager to another store. There are nine of us in this department, and our manager explained that she is going to watch us and see who has the greatest potential for the job. She will make her decision in the next three months. Now each of us is trying very hard to achieve recognition. There is so much tension that it's becoming impossible to come to work. How can I handle a situation like this without losing my temper?

ANSWER

You sound like a bunch of little kids trying to attract the attention of the teacher by outdoing each other at showing off. Give your boss a little more credit than that! She is watching you, presumably not looking for signs of your ability to grab attention but for your performance on the job—how you handle customers, coworkers, and high-pressure situations such as the one you now find yourself in. You can be certain that if you get the promotion that you are vying for, you'll have many more stressful situations ahead of you.

Don't be drawn into the whirlpool of destructive competition that may develop around you. Concentrate on your job. Do well, especially at those tasks that you would concentrate on if you were the assistant manager. Don't be too clever in trying to second-guess your manager—it will only backfire.

GIVE HONEST FEEDBACK TO ALL APPLICANTS

QUESTION

I interviewed several people who work elsewhere in our company for a higher-level secretarial position. Then I chose the individual I thought was best qualified for the job. Company policy and common courtesy required that I phone the other candidates to inform them of my decision and to thank them for their interest.

Nearly all these calls went well, but I encountered some rough spots. A few candidates asked why they were not selected. Should I simply have said that the person chosen best fit the needs of this job? Or do the unsuccessful candidates really want and deserve a fuller response, including a constructive critique of the strengths and weaknesses they would have brought to the job?

ANSWER

Take the extra time and effort and explain to all unsuccessful applicants why they weren't chosen. Then each can turn the process of applying for your opening into a learning experience. If they are short on certain skills or experience, by all means point that out. Doing so will help them, and since they are fellow employees you'll also be doing a service to the company.

The trick is to do this without discouraging the candidates. Don't be too brusque or matter-of-fact, but don't be apologetic either. Start by restating the skills that you were looking for and then compare those with that particular applicant's qualifications. Don't hesitate to acknowledge their strong points. Keep in mind, and remind the applicants if appropriate, that you had only *one* position to fill.

By explaining your thinking to the unsuccessful applicants, you will not only help their professional development, but you'll also be expressing respect for them. A brief answer devoid of details does quite the opposite.

MAKE THE APPLICANT FEEL BETTER OR GET BETTER?

My answer generated a rebuttal.

A reader felt that such an approach could easily degenerate into a defensive discussion about the applicant's shortcomings, and that it could also lead to a charge of discrimination in promotion.

His feeling was that the manager should merely reassure the applicants and refrain from discussing specific weaknesses, that it is best to avoid detail, just affirming instead that the candidate was indeed competitive.

I disagree with the drift of this comment. I think such an approach would be condescending and would dispense nothing more than topical medication to the applicants. It may make them *feel* better for the moment (and I even doubt this), but it won't help them *get* better.

To give real, lasting help to these candidates, one needs to point out areas of future improvement. Any discussion of these that doesn't also deal with their current capabilities will, by necessity, be superficial.

Regarding the suggestion that discussion of specifics could lead to charges of discrimination, I hate to see the already complex and challenging job of managing be made more so by constantly having to look over one's shoulder this way. Let's concentrate on doing what's *right!* It's hard enough.

• • •

One shouldn't be embarrassed about *wanting* a higher position—it's natural to have such ambitions. In pursuing them, I feel it's best if three simple rules are followed.

FIRST: APPLY FOR THE HIGHER JOB STRAIGHTFORWARDLY

QUESTION

I've been with my company for six months, and my boss has been with the company for three years. I do all of her work in addition to my own. She is getting promoted in a month, and I would like to get her current position. Do I tell our manager that I am doing all of my boss's work, or do I keep my mouth shut and hope he sees my qualifications and promotes me?

ANSWER

Apply for your boss's job in a straightforward manner. First, tell her that you'd love to have the job she will be leaving, and that you want to apply for it. Courtesy requires that you do so. In addition, you will need her support, as the manager will probably ask for her views. If, in fact, you have been doing her work, I see no reason why she won't support your application.

Then, ask for a meeting with the manager. Do your homework well. Think through in advance why you believe you are qualified for your boss's job in spite of your short tenure with the company, and then tell him. Describe, in specific terms, the work you have been doing but do *not* label it as your boss's work.

If, after all this, you still don't get promoted, don't be bitter. Find out from the manager why you were not chosen and, more importantly, what you should do to be a better candidate the next time such an opportunity comes your way.

SECOND: DON'T GO AROUND YOUR BOSS

QUESTION

How do I inform my manager that I can do a much better job than my immediate boss, the assistant manager? I don't want to cause personal conflict, but I'm yearning to show my talents.

ANSWER

If you think you are ready to do more work than you are now doing, ask the *assistant manager,* your own boss, for additional assignments. That will let you stretch your wings without generating conflict.

THIRD: LET CREDIT COME ON ITS OWN

QUESTION

I work for a rapidly growing company. Things have gotten quite busy lately, and my boss is giving me more and more of her work to do on top of the work that I already have. I enjoy doing the extra work, but I'm concerned that my efforts go unnoticed by top management.

How should I go about making sure I get credit for what I do?

ANSWER

Don't even try. Be happy that you get a chance to perform tasks you might not ordinarily be responsible for and use the opportunity to learn as much as possible of your boss's work. This experience will benefit you, maybe not immediately, but probably sooner than you think. Don't blow it by demanding credit—let it come on its own.

> There is a troubling element to promotions, too: One is always a bit worried about inadvertently following the cynical prescription of the Peter Principle—promoting a good worker to a level where he will not be able to perform well.
>
> In fact, this type of thing happens often. There is a cynical saying about how one loses the best salesman (or engineer or mechanic) by turning him into a mediocre manager. But what other choice is there? Should one promote a poor salesman (or engineer or mechanic)? Would that have a better chance of success? Not likely. Besides, what would that say to all the other salesmen (or engineers or mechanics)? Do a poor job—so you, too, can get promoted?
>
> The Peter Principle paradox is inevitable. We have no choice but to learn to deal with it.

GIVE A WORKER A TRYOUT AS SUPERVISOR

QUESTION

I am a department manager. I am considering promoting my most senior employee to a position where he would supervise about a third of my group. The problem is, I'm not sure if this person really will be able to handle the new responsibility.

He is a good individual worker but doesn't show the type of initiative and drive I think he'd need to succeed as a supervisor. On the one hand, I think I should give him a chance; on the other, I am afraid that if I promote him he will fail and I would need to let him go. Is there a way out of this dilemma?

ANSWER

There may be two ways out. First, you could discuss your reservations openly with your employee. Agree in advance that if you promote him, you will evaluate the situation, say, after six months. If you then find that your concerns have been justified, you will put him back into his previous role of individual worker (in which he had excelled). You can also agree that in that case you'd also take back any raise that may go with the promotion. Such a prior agreement can help remove the sting of failure. It will also help spell out what you expect from your employee in his job as a supervisor.

Another way would be to put your employee into the supervisory job on a temporary basis. Instead of promoting him formally, arrange things so he can do the job without a formal promotion at first. If he does well, you would go through with the promotion. Otherwise, his duties would revert to what they had been without any big trauma.

While I personally prefer the second approach—letting people try a job before they are promoted formally—both arrangements give a promising person a chance at advancement and at the same time provide a safety net if they don't make it. In any case, letting a good employee go because he fails in a new, higher-level job would be dead wrong.

HOW TO CORRECT A MISTAKE

QUESTION

Six months ago I promoted a loyal employee who has been with the company for twelve years to a management position. It appears now that his promotion was a real mistake. How should I deal with this situation? Firing him is not an option I want to consider.

ANSWER

You presumably made this selection because the employee did a good job in his previous assignment. I agree with you: Don't fire him now because he is not working out in a higher position. That's not only ethically wrong, but it would also deprive the company of the services of a proven good performer.

Instead, take a deep breath and face the mistake—his promotion—and rectify it in as objective and caring a way as you can.

Sit down with the employee and discuss your view of the situation. Be sure to include a recollection of the facts that led you to promote him in the first place: his prior good performance. Explain why you think he's not working out in his current position and then propose moving him back to his previous level.

Don't be embarrassed over this situation. You never know in advance how a person will perform in a job he or she has never done before. Consequently, every promotion involves risk, and some don't work out.

What *is* important is that you and the employee correct the error without damage to him or the company. The more objective you both are, the easier this will be to accomplish.

Part of the resolution of this problem is for you to find a position for this employee at the level where he performed well before his promotion and help him settle into it with dignity. In the future he may well be given another try at a promotion, with perhaps a better chance of success.

Such "recycling" of people is very logical. Since good performers are the ones chosen for promotion in the first place, saving them for the business and even for a future chance at a higher-level job is clearly worthwhile. Yet it's not practiced widely because most managers feel uncomfortable about proposing it to the prematurely promoted employee. To put it bluntly, it's easier to push such a person out the door, accompanied by the lame statement, "It just didn't work out . . ."

It doesn't have to be that way. Granted, proposing a lower-level job is not comfortable, but—excuse me for preaching—managers get paid to do what's *right,* not what's easy.

The first time I approached a subordinate with such a proposal I was very tense and nervous. He was sinking in his new job; we both knew it. Yet he had done very well in the years preceding his promotion. When he heard my proposal, he was visibly *relieved:* He had been girding himself for being fired. *He knew* that he was failing in his new position!

This happened fifteen years ago; the individual went on to a very successful career, eventually regaining and keeping the higher position.

LOOK AT YOUR PROMOTION FROM A COWORKER'S POINT OF VIEW

Not getting a promotion stirs up a lot of emotion. Others may have considered themselves candidates, and they won't relish losing out. Even those who knew that they weren't qualified for the higher position may not be cheering for the one who got it, particularly if they end up reporting to this person.

I think it helps if you can bring such feelings of resentment to the surface. Getting them out into the open may not make them go away, but at least it will put the dealings between the newly promoted manager and his previous peers on a more open and honest basis.

When I was named to my current position, I anticipated some negative reaction from the managers who had been my colleagues. After the announcement was made, I arranged to meet with each of them, one at a time. I asked how they felt about my promotion. Some said they thought it was well deserved and they looked forward to working with me. Others shrugged their shoulders and said something like it didn't bother them. One, however, plainly told me that he was not too happy; from what he knew of my management style, he didn't think he'd enjoy reporting to me. I swallowed hard and said something inane like I hoped we could work it out.

Yet this simple discussion helped clear the air between the two of us. We have now been working together for over twelve years and, after the first year or so, which was a bit contentious, we have gotten on extremely well.

QUESTION

I was recently promoted to a supervisory position, and I was really excited. However, my excitement was not shared by my coworkers. A couple of them have worked at the company longer than I have and are obviously jealous. They constantly give me a hard time and ignore my advice. It's affecting the output of the department that I'm now responsible for. What should I do to make them cooperate and lessen their hostility?

ANSWER

Try to see your promotion from the point of view of your coworkers who also wanted the job. Some resentment or jealousy is unavoidable in this situation, but it won't last long. Get on with the job and don't make the situation any worse.

Try not to respond to every real or imagined slight. Keep in mind that you too may be a bit insecure in your position and that you may be seeing resistance where there is none. If your co-workers reject your advice, ask them why—in an unemotional way. Let your work and reasoning dominate over sensitivities—yours or your employees'. And be patient. Time will help all of you to get used to your new roles.

FIND OUT WHY THE OTHER PERSON WAS CHOSEN, THEN DO SOMETHING ABOUT IT

Not being chosen when you think you should be provides more than a disappointment; it can bring self-doubts and, sometimes, a serious reexamination of one's career.

QUESTION

I was originally hired as a senior systems analyst; then three years ago I was given supervisory tasks. I gave my all to the job and received a very positive performance evaluation from my immediate supervisor.

Despite this, I've just been told that I've been a senior analyst all along and that supervising was just a "working assignment." I have also been assigned to another area with the possibility of a real promotion to a supervisory post with increased salary sometime next year.

Meanwhile, my former position was filled with an inexperienced younger person, and I am being asked to train and help him. I feel cheated and used. What should I do—gracefully accept everything and hope for the best? I am being paid very well.

QUESTION

I've been with my company for over three years. I consider myself to be well trained, competent, and fully experienced at my job. A month ago my former boss left the company. He was immediately replaced by a person who has only limited knowledge about our work.

I resent my new boss! Who is he to tell me how to do my job when I've been here longer and know how to do it better than he does? This has been very frustrating for me. I hope you can help me resolve the problem.

ANSWER

I'm going to deal with both of these questions together. Such predicaments are very common. Every time one person is chosen for a higher position, others around him or her are inevitably disappointed. In their own eyes, they are often better qualified for the job than the individual who was promoted. They're likely to be resentful toward both the person making the choice and the one who was chosen. Suspicions of favoritism may arise, and employees frequently leave, embittered by what took place.

Instead of reacting in this way, try to turn this event into an experience that can help you in the future. Assume that there were good reasons why another person was chosen over you and dedicate yourself to finding out what those reasons were. Only by doing that will you have a realistic hope of avoiding a repetition.

Ask for a meeting with the manager who made the choice. Explain that you were disappointed that you didn't get the promotion and indicate that you are very interested in getting the next one. You need a clear understanding of the factors that determined his previous choice. Ask for them, listen, and don't argue—no matter how tempted you may be. If you argue you will just cut the explanations short, and maybe stop the flow of valuable information.

After hearing the manager out, think long and hard about what you heard. Can you accept the values on which the choice was based? Do you still aspire to the job? Are you determined to acquire the skills and characteristics you would need? If the answer is yes, go to work on getting them. Knowing what you need to do should help focus your efforts and increase your chances of getting the next promotion.

If, on the other hand, you find that you cannot—or do not want to—acquire those capabilities, reexamine your plans and ambitions. Maybe you don't really want that promotion so badly. Or maybe you don't like the value system on which your employer based his choice. In that case, you probably should move on.

In any event, a thorough understanding of the thinking that went into the promotion can help you make a more intelligent decision about your own future. So ask, and listen well.

THE EMPLOYEE'S AND THE DEPARTMENT'S INTERESTS MUST BE BALANCED

The way these things often work in the real world, particularly in bigger organizations, is that the promotional opportunity will probably surface in a different department from the one in which you work. This gives your current boss a different role. While he undoubtedly wishes you well, your opportunity means a new problem for him. If you move on to take a higher position, he must find a replacement. So, that promotion is not quite yours yet . . .

QUESTION

I work at a large company as a manufacturing engineer. My supervisor relies heavily on me to solve problems on the production line. Recently I found out about an opening in our research department. I am qualified for the job and I think it would give me a real growth opportunity. The trouble is, my boss says he needs me and won't let me go. This is terribly frustrating. What should I do?

ANSWER

Your desire and need for advancement must be weighed against your current department's interest. I suspect neither you nor your boss are in a good position to do that objectively; you need the help of an impartial third party.

Ask your boss for an opportunity to appeal his decision to *his* manager, who is likely to be a bit more detached from the immediate needs of the production line and can consider the pros and cons of your move from a broader perspective.

After such an appeal, if you still aren't allowed to move, you should work out a plan of action with your boss (for instance, training a replacement) that would allow you to take advantage of such an opportunity the next time it comes up.

Sometimes employees have all the qualifications they need for higher jobs but won't get them because they are too closely identified with the role they now play at their company. For instance, a person who started work as a production worker or as a secretary may forever be typecast in those roles in the eyes of the higher-ups. This image may stay with the individual even after he or she completes further education.

This is a tough barrier to break. In some cases it may be easier to move on to another company, where the employee does not carry the burden of the prior image.

16

Coworkers on Your Nerves

OUR coworkers are usually very important to us. Our activities at work are almost always connected with theirs. To do our work well, we are dependent on them and they are on us. The people we work with are a major factor in determining whether or not our workplace is pleasant and congenial—maybe even fun! More often than not, our feelings toward the people we work with are crucial in determining if we *like* going to work each morning.

So, it's not surprising that problems with coworkers, even if they are minor in nature, can significantly affect our own work and, indeed, the work of our entire group. Sorting out such problems is important for the benefit of our productivity, as well as for our own emotional well-being.

I advocate handling coworker problems *directly* with them. Third parties are worse than useless in such conflicts: They become an audience for whom the principals play their roles. It's best to confine the discussion to the *specific* complaint you have and to avoid generalizations like "you *always* this . . . and *never* that . . ."

NEXT TIME THEY START CHATTING, ASK THEM TO STOP

QUESTION

I work at a busy computerized public library with a number of college-age people. They carry on long, distracting conversations during work when we are all supposed to be checking books in and out on the computer. Their chatting increases the probability of errors. How should I approach my somewhat apathetic boss with this serious potential problem of customer relations?

ANSWER

You shouldn't approach your poor boss about this problem at all—he has better things to do. Next time the chatting starts, just turn to your coworkers and tell them very straightforwardly that their conversation makes it difficult for you to do your work. Then, equally straightforwardly, ask if they would please stop.

HOW TO TELL YOUR COLLEAGUE THAT HE IS MESSING UP

Problems with coworkers can be a lot more serious than too much chatting, but the approach to take is similar.

QUESTION

I'm one of five department managers reporting to the general manager of a division of a fairly large company. I am the youngest and also the most junior department manager. One of my more senior peers is just "out of it." He displays a noticeable lack of interest at meetings; he delegates to his subordinates so extensively that he's unaware of even the very basic aspects of major projects under him, and he refuses to make a decision on anything, even minor matters, unless he has first checked with every person on his staff (which takes days).

The rest of the organization works around him, but he's a big drain on productivity. The work somehow gets done, but the fundamental problem remains: The managerial function that he should be performing for his group is missing. I'm concerned; I'd like to talk to him, but because of my junior role I'm afraid he'll totally disregard my input. How can I approach him and get him to listen?

ANSWER

You have to focus more closely on your own role in this situation. First and foremost, you are responsible for the work done by *your* own department. This is completely and legitimately your concern. The overall performance of your colleague, however, is not—it is the concern of your boss, the general manager.

If your colleague's lack of involvement in his job is making it difficult for you to do yours, that is a problem you can and should address directly with him. Ask him for a one-on-one meeting; your problem is too complex to be dealt with in a casual encounter.

In the meeting with your colleague, be specific in describing how he is hindering you and what actions you would like him to take. Ask him to commit himself to fixing these specifics.

Your approach should be aimed at solving your specific problem, not at correcting your peer's performance. If this orientation is clear in your dealings with your colleague, you will greatly increase your chances of accomplishing something useful.

Note that I suggest a *one-on-one* meeting as the medium in which to approach the troublesome colleague. It works here for the same reason that it works as the best way for boss and employee to interact: It provides focused, intense exposure, which is a must if you are dealing with a difficult subject. The mere act of arranging such a meeting with a colleague will probably telegraph to him that you have something important to discuss, and may cause him to think things over in advance.

A TACTFUL LETTER CAN RESOLVE A PERSONAL CONFLICT

If the problem is particularly sensitive, you may want to use a *letter* to state your position. On difficult subjects, this may be easier than going through a face-to-face confrontation. Your colleague may also find it less traumatic to read your complaints in privacy, with no need for an immediate response. A subsequent face-to-face meeting may be a lot more productive after your coworker has had a chance to digest the contents of your letter.

QUESTION

I recently started to work for a small company. One of my coworkers was assigned to teach me all about the project that I was given.

After a month, I developed some improvements and was given more responsibility. Unfortunately, my original mentor is now hostile and resentful. In fact, he has deliberately created problems to make my job more difficult.

I have confronted him with my observations, trying to work out a civil relationship, but in vain. I'd like to resolve my problem without bringing it to the attention of our boss—I really don't want to create any more resentment. What should I do?

ANSWER

Your choices are limited. You have already confronted your mentor, without success, and you don't want to go to your boss. Approach your mentor one more time, but set the stage for involving your boss if matters between the two of you don't improve.

One way to do this would be through a letter addressed to your mentor. In it, acknowledge the help you received from him when you started to work at the company and describe the problem that has developed. Be specific; describe incidents that support your claim that he is deliberately trying to make your job more difficult. Refer back to your earlier attempt to work out your problems. Stress that you are dedicated to making the relationship productive and solicit your mentor's view about anything *you* might be doing to cause the problem. Finally, suggest that if you can't work matters out, you should approach your boss *together*.

Such a letter should give your mentor sufficient incentive to be open about any resentment he has toward you (he may, after all, have some valid reasons), and could give the impetus to start to rebuild a healthy working relationship between the two of you.

The strange thing about personal conflicts at work is that, over time, little irritations can build up into what are *felt* to be major conflicts. Some time ago, a person whose job required him to spend a lot of time on transatlantic telephone calls was moved near me at work. The nature of his job, combined with his naturally loud speaking voice, shattered my peace and quiet. (Remember, I work in an open office setup, surrounded by five-foot-high partitions.)

I sat in my office, increasingly annoyed by the loud voice that reached me over the partition. Finally, and only after I waited too long, I approached the fellow with my complaint, angrily and stiffly. He was taken aback but apologized and promised to watch his decibels.

I wish I could end this story with the statement that we both worked happily next to each other forever after, but that was not the case. My neighbor's voice crept back up, despite several reminders from me. Interestingly, these were much easier to make in the wake of my original discussion with him. (Eventually, I ended up using the privileges of my rank, and he moved to another office, further away.)

The moral of the story:

DON'T LET (GUM-CRACKING) MOLEHILLS BECOME MOUNTAINS

QUESTION

I was recently hired into an accounting department. My problem is that the woman who works at the desk next to mine is a habitual gum chewer. This in itself wouldn't bother me, except for the fact that she cracks it constantly. I find this very distracting, but being the new kid on the block, I don't want to make any waves. Is there a tactful way to resolve this situation?

ANSWER

I am afraid there's only one way to handle this problem: You need to deal with your coworker directly. She probably has no idea that her habit is noticed by anyone else, let alone that it's distracting.

Be gentle in your approach. Take her aside, perhaps during a break, and start out by introducing the subject with a bit of an apology. After all, it's a personal habit of hers that you intend to discuss. Stress the *effect* her gum chewing has on your ability to do your job—this is what makes it legitimate for you to raise the issue in the first place.

Don't wait too long, or your frustration and anger could build up so much that you might start the discussion with an outburst. That would not be fair nor would it lead to the desired result.

IF THEY BOTHER YOU, LET THEM KNOW

When it comes to ways in which people can get on their coworkers' nerves, there seems to be no limit. Otherwise innocuous personal habits can get magnified by a lot of exposure at close proximity. I have seen people get worked up over smoking—and over others' annoyed reaction to their smoke; over whistling, munching, or messy offices. I've seen people irritated by their coworkers who were excited about their upcoming wedding, or started the day off with a moody expression; by those who give verbose answers to questions and by those who are taciturn. The list just goes on.

In all cases, when the irritation builds up and you feel an urge to take action, there is no better way to handle it than by a direct discussion.

QUESTION

Help! We work in an office that has open-office landscaping. The noise level usually isn't too bad, but we have a problem with two new employees who constantly spit. One of them can be heard all over the building!

At least four of us are really bothered by this, and we don't know how to approach the two men. We don't want to go up to them and say, "Please quit spitting."

It also seems like a petty thing to go to their managers about. Do you have any suggestions on how we can politely let these men know that their habit is making us sick?

ANSWER

I see no other way to get them to stop doing something that bothers you than letting them know that it does. The trick is to do it without embarrassing them or creating a problem that's worse than their spitting habit.

Write a polite letter to your coworkers telling them how their habit affects you and asking them to refrain from spitting in the office. Sign the letter—you really have nothing to be ashamed of and shouldn't act like you do.

Don't expect miracles—habits like this die very slowly. They are second nature to your coworkers, so they probably don't even notice when they are doing it. Be prepared to remind them from time to time—again through brief, gentle notes.

17
Friends and Family at Work: Must Keep Everything in Their Proper Compartments

WE spend an enormous part of our waking hours at the workplace. We have a great deal in common with our colleagues—we work side by side with them, we have lunch together, we bitch about the same boss, and we gossip about the person in the next cubicle . . . It's little wonder then that we end up making friends at work and that the people we work with are important to us.

Yet . . .

FRIENDS AT THE WORKPLACE CAN SPELL TROUBLE AND COMPLICATIONS

QUESTION

I work in a small office where the manager and the employees deal informally with each other on a daily basis. When the manager must take stern measures with his employees—who are also his friends—problems arise. How can he maintain respect without damaging these friendships?

QUESTION

During my four years at a firm, I've become a close friend of one of the company's top executives. Recently the company hired a manager for the division I work in. He reports to my friend. Unfortunately, my friendship is creating an uncomfortable situation because my new boss treats me awkwardly, fearing that I will run to my friend with observations about his performance. Fellow employees tell me that he frequently comments about my friendship with his boss behind my back. I feel that the problem stems from my new boss's insecurity; still, I'd like to alleviate the situation. What should I do?

QUESTION

I was recently promoted to a supervisory position. I now find myself in a tricky situation: I supervise someone who is a personal friend. She finds it difficult to take instructions from me; she always argues before giving in. I'm afraid my new position will end our friendship. What can I do to minimize these bad feelings? I also wonder if the position is worth destroying a friendship for.

As these questions indicate, having friendships in the workplace can be a bag of worms. There are several schools of thought on this subject, most of them prescribing who it is OK to be friends with. For instance, a manager I know told me that he would socialize only with people on his own level. He felt that having friends either at a higher or lower level would only lead to problems—a point of view that is certainly supported by the above letters. I have trouble with this approach; it implies that you must rearrange your friendships with every promotion or reorganization.

Another, more radical approach is based on the belief that friends and work just don't mix. Proponents of this view simply avoid socializing and making friends with their coworkers. To me, this removes one of the more pleasant elements of work: to engage in common activities with people whose company you enjoy. It seems like an extremely costly solution to the problem at hand.

I believe we should dedicate ourselves to making friendships and work *coexist*. Decide firmly in your mind that you will be friends with whomever you like, regardless of their position at the workplace, but that you will also do what you must in order to do your job well, without regard to your friendships. Your basic outlook is critical. If you believe that you cannot manage friendships at work, you definitely won't be able to. If, on the other hand, you approach the situation convinced that it *can* work, then chances are that you *will* succeed.

I'm not suggesting for a moment that it will be easy. It will often require careful thought about what's right, as well as a strong will and self-discipline. But I'm convinced that it's worth it.

This is my answer to the three readers.

ANSWER

When a manager has friends among his employees and stern measures are called for, he will just have to take a deep breath and—mustering objectivity and determination—say and do those difficult things that the situation requires.

If you are friendly with your boss's boss, you must be totally meticulous in your dealings with both of them. Maintain your friendship but never gossip about your boss with your friend. Resolve your work problems with your own boss, never involving your friend. Tell your boss clearly that you plan to live by these rules. With strict adherence to them, everyone will eventually learn to live with the situation.

No advancement is worth the destruction of a friendship, but I also feel that such an outcome need not be. Both the new supervisor (the third writer) and his employee-friend can learn to deal with the change in their status. This will take time and effort from both. The new supervisor should take the lead. Arrange a meeting with your friend at a place and time where you can have a lengthy discussion without distractions.

Start off by telling about your discomfort at the turn your relationship has taken and that you intend to do whatever is necessary to make both relationships work. Ask for her views and try to understand your friend's perspective. It's possible that your own awkwardness over this situation has made you act in ways you shouldn't—and probably wouldn't—with your other employees.

NAH, JUST TRANSFER THE EMPLOYEE

Not everybody agrees with this approach. My answer elicited a rather strong rebuttal from a reader.

A READER'S RESPONSE

Come on! This is *not* a situation that is going to be solved by frank talk. The person who wrote is now making more money. He is now going to meetings his friend isn't attending. He's talking to higher-level managers on a different basis.

Your answer doesn't represent reality. Tell it like it is! Businesses are jungles. There are people who would sell their own grandmother down the river for a promotion.

I would simply suggest transferring the employee as a matter of course.

ANSWER

Some businesses are jungles. Most are decent, fair places to work. *Some* people would sacrifice their friendships for a promotion. (They would, for instance, do as you suggest: transfer their friends out of the area in order *not* to have to deal with the change in their relationship.) Others would put their energy into reconciling personal and work relationships and making both work.

You seem to want me to say how bad it can be, but I'm telling it the way it *should* be—and can be—if common sense and ordinary decency prevail.

Over the years, I have dealt successfully with such situations and I've seen many colleagues do likewise.

One situation involved a coworker who became my friend. He didn't report directly to me, but we worked together on many projects. One day he decided to leave the company. There weren't any particular problems, just the lure of another opportunity. His departure came at the worst possible time for our company. It left a major hole and disrupted progress in a pretty bad way.

I was stunned by his decision, resented it, and felt betrayed. While my friend clearly had made up his mind to leave, he also felt quite guilty about it. After he left, we both made real efforts to keep our relationship going. At first our contacts were very awkward—one of us resentful, the other guilt-ridden. But time dampened those feelings, and gradually our friendship returned to normal.

A couple of years later I realized that he wasn't happy in his new position. I signaled our company's openness to have him come back. Nothing came of it for a while, but eventually we started to talk more about it and, in fact, he eventually returned. Our personal friendship, which survived the work crisis, was actually helpful in working out his return to the company.

I'm not unique in this. I know a group of three managers who have been personal friends for years. Among other things, they've developed a tradition of going together on annual skiing vacations. Over the years, the reporting relationship among these three underwent several changes: Peers became boss and employee, and, in one case, a supervisory relationship was even reversed. The personal friendships continued through all these changes and their work relationship remained excellent.

However, despite the best of intents, sometimes things don't work out. I have also seen situations where, in spite of considerable effort, work conflicts have damaged—even destroyed—personal relationships. Still, these are far outnumbered by cases of successful coexistence.

KEEP FAMILY AND WORK RELATIONSHIPS
METICULOUSLY SEPARATE

If friendships are difficult to reconcile in the work environment, family relationships pose even greater challenges. Here, I'm not as optimistic that a successful outcome can be reached. Yet the prescription of how to go about it is the same: Keep each relationship in its own separate place, its own "compartment." Do not let the status of one influence the status of the other.

QUESTION

My mother is the owner of a small service firm. My brother, who lives at home, works for her. They both bring their work problems home, so I hear nothing else discussed there. What is worse, my brother insists on telling our mother how to run the business, and she resents it. So, they bicker all the time.

Is it good for my brother to continue to work for our mother?

QUESTION

I have worked for a large grocery chain for some time. Recently I tried to get my brother a job with the company. I was told it was against company policy for relatives to work at the same location. If my brother is to work for the company, it would have to be clear across town from me—a real inconvenience.

Is such a policy legal? Even if it's legal, is it a good practice?

ANSWER

These questions illustrate just two of the many complexities that arise when relatives work together. Fortunately, as far as I know, the law stays away from this question, so each firm can formulate its own policies. My own feeling is that for both relationships—the one on the job and the one in the family—to work, one must keep them *meticulously separate*. That's difficult if there is a supervisor/subordinate relationship between relatives. (How would you like to have to write a performance review about the work of your spouse!) So, most organizations have rules that prevent that situation, and rightly so.

Small, privately owned companies like the service firm referred to in the first question frequently don't have such rules and they often employ members of the owner's family. I don't think that's good practice either for the junior member of the family (the son in this case) or for the firm. The family member will never be sure of the measure of his merit (how can he know if he'd hold the same position if he were not the owner's son?). Getting along at work is hard enough without piling such ambiguities on the employee's shoulders. It would be far better if the son could first prove himself in an outside firm before joining the family business.

Some organizations, like the grocery chain referred to in the second question, go overboard and prohibit relatives from working in the same office or store altogether. This may save the manager in charge from having to deal with some problems, like, for instance, two relatives spending too much time socializing with each other at work. However, I think such problems are minor, and a manager should be able to handle them without the crutch of a "no relatives" policy.

SHOULD THEY BE PUNISHED FOR BEING MARRIED?

The absurdity of some "solutions" to the relatives-at-work problem are illustrated by the following exchange.

QUESTION

I manage a department in a medium-size company. Recently I hired a person who used to live in New England. He moved to the West Coast to come to work for us. His wife is a professional person with skills that our company (not my department) has been looking for. I suggested to the appropriate manager that he should interview her. The problem is, our personnel department won't let him. They feel it's not a good practice to have husband and wife both work for the same company. Is that a good rule?

ANSWER

I don't agree with such a policy. While there might be problems of real or perceived favoritism in cases where relatives supervise each other, I can't see any point in depriving a company of the services of a good person just because the spouse also works there. Surely you wouldn't prohibit the hiring of two people who live together. Should you then punish them for being married?

THE SON WILL END UP RUNNING THE BUSINESS

Even if *you* are not related to the owner, working for a family-owned company has its unique set of problems.

QUESTION

For the past seven years, I've been the plant manager of a thirty-year-old food service company. The business is owned and operated by a husband-and-wife team who have managed to maintain a close-knit family atmosphere in the company.

Now that the business is firmly established, the owners tend to leave it in the hands of their son while they travel. The problem is, the son has no management capabilities. Consequently, when the owners are gone, many employees come to me dissatisfied and threatening to quit unless I speak to them about their son. Should I? How?

ANSWER

As a senior management-level employee, you have a responsibility both to the other employees and to the owners to do something about a bad situation that has the potential of getting worse. So, yes, I think you should confront this issue, and soon.

I also think you should take great pains to do so constructively: After all, it's likely that the son will end up running the business sooner or later. Your aim should be to induce the owners to prepare their son now for his upcoming responsibility.

Collect the evidence carefully: What exactly does he do wrong? Jot down your thoughts, along with examples—the more the better. When you're ready, ask for a private meeting with the owners. Tell them in advance that the subject is sensitive. Present your case, stressing that your aim is to make sure their son receives the right training so that he can run the business in the tradition they have established.

Come to this meeting with some suggestions on how to train him. Does he lack knowledge of the business? Maybe he would profit from hands-on assignments under the supervision of the parents. Does he lack understanding of finance? Maybe he should enroll in a suitable course . . . and so on.

The point is, by making a few constructive suggestions, you will set the tone of the discussion to indicate that you are searching for a solution to a very important and sensitive problem. This should help prevent the session from degenerating into just a pointless or hostile bitch session.

AT FAMILY FIRMS, YOU ARE SUBJECT TO THE BOSS'S WHIM

QUESTION

I am a secretary at a small firm. Recently, my boss's daughter called the office and asked if I would type a college paper for her. I said no. She politely said thank you and good-bye.

The next day my boss told me that he expected me to do his daughter's typing. I answered that I did not feel that such chores were part of my job, that I do not type for my own teenage children and that I thought his daughter, too, should be able to type her own college work. We discussed this for a while but came to no agreement.

Two days later my boss came to my desk and handed me a check, telling me that I was being let go because of a recent decrease in his business. I asked if this decision had anything to do with our difference of opinion about typing his daughter's college papers. He said no. I told him I didn't believe that. He then said I could believe what I wanted, but that I was to be out of the office at the end of that day.

Later I found out that my job went to his daughter. I worked for this man for eight years and never had any problems. I feel that I have been treated unfairly. What do you think of this situation?

ANSWER

Working for a small, owner-run company has its drawbacks. Larger organizations have rules, written or otherwise, regarding what is acceptable conduct by managers and employees.

These rules provide common expectations for all. Such rules do not exist in small firms headed by the owner. Here, the boss's power to hire, fire, reward, and punish is virtually unlimited.

At a large company, I would consider the treatment meted out to you outrageous. There you would have had a job description that detailed what you were expected to do in your job; typing papers for the boss's daughter would not have been listed there. Not only that, many companies have explicit rules prohibiting the use of secretaries for a supervisor's personal chores. Additionally, you could have taken your problem to your boss's boss, or to the personnel people.

In the small, owner-managed firm where you worked, the rules were, simply, set by the boss. If you didn't like them, your only alternative was to leave—but the outcome of a show of force was totally predictable.

Friendships, relationships, and relatives on the one hand, and promotions, reporting relationships, and work conflicts on the other will certainly complicate the already difficult human interactions at the workplace. But the prescription to make it all work is simple even if doing it is difficult: Keep everything in its proper compartment. This applies to all the different types of give-and-take you'll encounter at work.

WHATEVER THE GOSSIP, TREAT YOUR RELATIVE LIKE ANY OTHER EMPLOYEE

QUESTION

A few months ago I started working at a local firm. I got the job through a relative who works there. Unfortunately, I learned from my fellow employees that he is having an affair. Should I speak to his wife about this situation? My fellow employees don't want to get involved, but they're not related to him. I'm concerned.

ANSWER

You landed this job with the help of your relative, but now that you work there, you should think of yourself as any other employee. You probably work hard to earn your salary and do the best you can without any undue reliance or help from your relative. I think you should adopt the same attitude when it comes to your relative's private conduct at the workplace—treat your relative no differently than you would anybody else at work.

I doubt that you would run to tell another coworker's wife about whatever rumors are circulating. So whatever you may think about your relative's personal conduct, you should close an imaginary door on it every time you leave your workplace. Your relationship at work is one thing, your relationship outside of it is another; the only way you can keep both healthy is by keeping them strictly separate.

18
Women in the Workplace: No Longer Separate, But Not Yet Equal

TODAY the presence of women in the workplace provides new problems to all concerned. While women have always been present, they now appear in new capacities. They are engineers, crawling under complex machinery. They are law enforcement officers, riding with fellow officers in patrol cars. And they are managers. In short, women have penetrated the work environment in roles that until a few years ago were solely filled by men. The new roles bring with them new problems.

THEY WON'T TREAT ME AS ONE OF THEM

QUESTION

I am the only female in a work group of four. The other three members of the group are not used to working with women and they don't treat me as one of them. They exclude me from their activities and even from their conversations. What should I do to become accepted?

ANSWER

There is very little you *can* do. In fact, the harder you try to become "one of the boys," the more likely it is that a distance will remain between you and the rest of the group. All I can suggest is that you shrug your shoulders and go about doing your work. As time goes on, they will get used to you and the barriers will gradually weaken.

When women first appear in a new line of work—for instance, in management—they are greeted with a cautious, awkward attitude by the men around them. We simply don't quite know how to act, we don't know what we can and can't say; suddenly we become self-conscious.

The first such experience I recall was when a woman joined a management group that up till then had consisted of only males. Our group generally used salty, occasionally even profane, language without giving it a second thought. After this woman joined us, we tried to clean up our language, assuming that our usual style would be offensive to her. This cleanup attempt led to so much stammering and half-uttered phrases followed by clumsy apologies that the spontaneity and quality of our discussions clearly deteriorated.

The woman in our midst at first acted as if she noticed nothing. After a while, when this clumsy situation continued, she told us to stop acting like a bunch of schoolchildren around the principal; she threatened that if we didn't talk as we did before, *she'd* start using the type of language we had been trying to avoid. This comment helped some; still, it took months before we could be truly comfortable with her presence.

This type of situation seems altogether typical. Worse, it often involves weightier matters.

TO BREAK THE GENDER BARRIER, ACT SLOWLY BUT PERSISTENTLY

QUESTION

I am a woman in a responsible management position. I happen to be the only female manager in my department, and therein lies the root of my problem.

My department has weekly meetings that typically involve "brainstorming" sessions where we come up with ways to deal with various business issues. I contribute as much to these meetings as my associates, and yet my suggestions are passed over for those of the men. I'm afraid if I call my boss on this, he'll think that I'm behaving like a "feminist."

Should I grin and bear it or do something about it?

ANSWER

It's a little hard to answer this question without knowing how long you've been a member of this all-male group. If you've just joined it recently, my suggestion is to wait. These men have been meeting for a long time without a woman in their midst, and given some time, they may very well get used to your presence and start treating you as an equal.

Meanwhile, make notes on your suggestions that are ignored. If the situation doesn't improve as time goes on, you'll need specifics to support your complaint. Approach your boss privately with the list. Present your case and stress that not only is your pride hurt, but also that your employer is being deprived of the benefit of your ideas—something for which he pays you.

It's very important to make your boss realize that what you say is really happening. If you can get him to alter *his* behavior toward you, the ice will be broken and the others in the group will follow his lead.

However, even if he earnestly commits to improving matters, don't expect immediate and lasting change. Behavior based on habits of many years changes slowly. So, be persistent.

PRESS TO HAVE YOUR CONTRIBUTIONS HEARD

It's easier for me, a male manager, to counsel patience and persistence than it is for a woman manager pursuing a career to accept it. She's bound to be less philosophical about the extra obstacles in her way. One of my readers added her own voice to my answer, arguing that *impatience* can be a virtue.

COMMENT

I read your recent column about the woman manager whose boss and peers (all men) totally overlook her comments and input in meetings.

I am a woman and have been a software supervisor at a large corporation for the last six years. I've experienced the same problems and I would like to share my experience with your readers.

I first tried, as you suggested, to wait and see if time would bring acceptance. This didn't work at all. The men I worked with simply didn't respect my opinion. Next, much as you suggested, I wrote up my complaints and had a meeting with my boss. That helped only slightly, and his attitude change did not spread to the rest of the group. But I wasn't going to let either my boss or my peers off the hook. So I came up with a tactic that turned out to be most helpful and was missing from your answer.

Whenever I can see that a suggestion or opinion of mine is being ignored, I press to have my contributions heard. I stop my boss or my peer and confront the situation professionally and without emotion.

I'll say, "Look, I just made a suggestion, and you totally ignored it." I will do this even in public. People have gotten the message that they'd better not overlook me and my suggestions unless they are prepared to be confronted openly and can defend their actions.

I think I'm beginning to be viewed in a new light.

HAND HER A BOX OF TISSUES—AND LISTEN

It's important to stress that most of us men are not deliberately out to "keep women in their place." We often just don't quite know how to deal with situations that we have not had to face before.

Here is an example.

QUESTION

I have a female employee. Quite often, in the course of resolving various business situations, she'll begin to cry.

I really have a very difficult time with this. My male reaction is to try to comfort her, while my professional response dictates that I remain unemotional and wait for the storm to end.

After each of these incidents, I am irritated by her behavior and I feel manipulated. I don't know how to separate my male reaction from my professional one comfortably.

ANSWER

First of all, try to understand that crying is just one more manifestation of emotion. It simply happens to be one you are not used to.

You probably have less trouble dealing with more familiar emotional expressions—signs of annoyance or frustration—than with tears. So, when you next encounter tears, tell yourself, "She (or he) is upset. I'll have to figure out why." Hand your employee a box of tissues, lean back, and listen.

AVOID A BIG STINK: SEEK DEMONSTRABLE FAIRNESS IN PAY

But getting used to the presence of women at the workplace is only one matter. There is also the issue of pay. While lawyers and courts struggle with abstract concepts like "comparable worth," women at work face daily conflicts about how to deal with a real or perceived double standard in the pay scale. At the risk of alienating my impatient female readers, I counsel solutions which are more practical if they are less rapid. I believe that the shape a long-term career takes always outweighs next year's pay in importance.

I have seen instances in which a pay inequity took on a significance and life of its own. The employee who felt slighted got so emotionally involved with the specific pay issue that she put its immediate resolution ahead of all other considerations. It became a momentous, all-consuming cause for her, and other aspects of her career—like her relations with her supervisor and peers and even her performance on the job—became secondary. The result was a lose/lose situation in which, even though she won the skirmish, the employee, her work, and her boss all suffered.

Steady pressure, based on facts and reasoning, is likelier to bring about the desired outcome without damaging everything else in the process.

QUESTION

I have been offered a promotion for which I've worked very hard. My problem is that a male coworker who has the same job I've been offered is making significantly more than I will be if I decide to take the job. I want this position but I want to be paid a wage comparable to my male counterpart. How should I go about this? I'm afraid that if I make a big stink, I won't get the job.

ANSWER

You are right. Making a big stink before you get the job could very well mean you won't get the promotion at all. And taking the job and then making a big stink would result in ill feelings toward you at a time when you most need your boss's help and goodwill.

Accept the promotion graciously. Go to work in your new position, put your best effort into the job, and produce results. If, after you have a track record, you feel you are still unfairly compensated, address the issue with your supervisor and a compensation specialist, if there is one in your company.

Support your approach with as many facts as you can. Don't base your case on a comparison with just one other individual; that may lead to erroneous conclusions. Maybe that person has considerably stronger qualifications, more experience, or simply has a better performance record than you. Ask to be shown how you are paid in comparison to others in your category. Your aim should be to ask for demonstrable fairness, rather than a specific dollar adjustment. That's what will serve you best in the long term.

And, of course, with men and women working side by side, sexuality will be more evident at the workplace. A relatively innocuous manifestation:

CONCENTRATE ON WORK, EVEN IF YOUR COLLEAGUE IS FLIRTATIOUS

QUESTION

I am a woman. I work for a large computer firm and I'll be considered for promotion in the near future. However, another woman, who is also being considered for the same position, is more friendly and flirtatious with our boss. What can I do to get this promotion without compromising my values?

ANSWER

I certainly don't think you should go into competition with your coworker in the area of flirtatiousness! Concentrate on your work. Stress the characteristics that have made you a candidate for promotion, and keep a good attitude. If you get the promotion, great; if you don't, don't undermine your coworker or become sour. After all, you can't be sure that her flirtatiousness had anything to do with the outcome.

More problematic is the inevitable mine field that a woman has to walk through in making her way in a world where much—really, most—of the power and influence is in male hands.

YOUNG, FEMALE, AND BLOND—AND "HIT ON"

QUESTION

About a year ago I started my own company. My problem is that I'm young, female, and blond. Almost every time I deal with a male client I'm "hit on."

I want to be nice, but it's pretty hard to be nice to someone who talks to my breasts instead of my face. Is there an approach that successful businesswomen use to overcome this obstacle?

This question really stumped me. Frankly, I was uncomfortable answering it because not only did I not know *what* to say, but also I suddenly became very aware of my maleness. I asked for help:

ANSWER

Not being young, blond, or female, I find myself unqualified to give you suggestions that have been proven valid in real life. I'd like to appeal to businesswomen among my readers. Please write and tell me how you have been coping with this problem.

I got a strong response to my plea, all from women, yet representing quite a number of approaches and attitudes. Here is a sample.

READERS' RESPONSES

I am female. As a business attorney, I deal with many men, and as a member of several women's business associations, I've talked with many women about this problem. The only approach that's effective without risking the loss of a client is humor. Depending on what the woman is comfortable with, the humor can range from ribald and direct to soft and subtle. Of course, it's best if a woman can truly view the situation as funny and come up with a spontaneous, appropriate comeback. However, many younger women often need to prepare a few one-liners in advance.

• • •

How you react to overtures is the key to how you'll be treated by men. In a sense they are testing you. If you find their comments and behavior amusing, they'll take that as encouragement. If you want to discourage this treatment, give my method a try.

When men "come on" to me, I simply and tactfully explain that I'm flattered by their interest, but I'm not interested in that type of relationship. It's important to be consistent. Don't turn a man down for a date and then flash him a coy smile as you leave.

If you want to detract attention from your figure, dress accordingly. Men will stare at you if you give them something to stare at. Save the tight sweaters and low-cut blouses for social occasions. Choose clothing that's flattering yet doesn't accent the sexual side of your personality. Some men may still look at you, even in your conservative attire, but they're less likely to ogle.

• • •

If a man is distracted from what a woman is saying, a subtle response might be sufficient to get his attention back. A slightly more direct approach is to say something like, "I know you don't mean to be offensive, but I feel uncomfortable when someone doesn't look me in the eye."

• • •

The fact is, you have to be prepared to work with men; you must prepare yourself each morning to expect new misunderstandings that day. Don't be defensive and wait for a fight, but don't be taken by surprise either.

You must be professional. A woman who does not act like a professional can't blame anyone else for her problems. You have no control over how you are treated by others. But you can control how you act.

• • •

The self-description the letter writer offers, "young and blond," serves as a starting place. A person's self-perception carries over into the manner in which others perceive her. If she sees herself primarily as young and attractive, that's how she will subconsciously present herself to clients.

She should approach a client with a mental attitude that says, "I am a professional, capable and competent." When this self-perception is underscored by dress and mannerisms that denote professional strength, rather than an attitude of "I'm nice; like me, please," clients will cease to see her as someone who can be "hit on" because she no longer is vulnerable.

• • •

In reply to the young lady, I offer the following. Twenty-five years ago I found myself in a similar situation, feeling the same way. However, from where I sit today, I would advise you to enjoy the "problem." Nature has a way of overcoming such obstacles by changing our attitudes (not to mention our figures). By the time you reach my age, you'll awaken one day reflecting fondly on those memories and wonder where your "problems" went.

THE LAW CAN STOP HARASSMENT, BUT IT WON'T PROVIDE A GOOD WORK ENVIRONMENT

Women aren't the only victims of those who try to use commercial influence to gain sexual favors—*men* can also face the same problem. With the increased legitimacy of homosexuality, its open presence at the workplace has increased as well.

QUESTION

I am a heterosexual male. I am new at my job, but in the few weeks that I've been here, I've been propositioned by two men, both my immediate supervisors. Outside of work I would know how to handle such a situation—it's happened before. How do I handle it in this case?

ANSWER

Make up your mind *firmly and unequivocally* that—work or not, boss or not—in personal matters you will do exactly what you want to do, nothing more and nothing less. Before anybody else will believe what you tell them, *you* must be very clear of your intent. Then the next time you're approached, tell your boss that you are not interested. Say it calmly and seriously, and add a request that he not bring the subject up again, as it makes you uncomfortable.

If your boss approaches you again, reject him again in the same way, but immediately sit down and write him a letter. Start by explaining that your purpose in writing is to avoid any possible misunderstanding between the two of you. Describe the above incidents, explain your feelings of discomfort, and repeat your desire that these approaches stop. Seeing his conduct described in the black and white of written language may make your boss stop, even if he could rationalize your verbal rejections away.

Once you write such a letter, the atmosphere at your workplace will probably be affected—perhaps permanently. There may be recriminations against you, in which case you may want to ask for the help of your human-resource organization or even seek legal help; after all, sexual harassment is against the law. Your situation is no different from that of a woman rejecting the advances of a male supervisor.

However, keep in mind that while the law can stop harassment, it cannot provide a good work environment. More than likely, the working relationship between you and your boss will become strained and uncomfortable. If so, there may be very little you can do about it, and your best bet may then be to look for a job elsewhere. Life is too short to be spent working for a boss who harbors a resentment against you.

19

What Is Right?

IF your boss tells you to work on project A ahead of project B, you'll probably accept his authority to set your priorities. When he shows you the way he wants you to put together a customer presentation, you'll undoubtedly heed his input. But sometimes you may encounter situations in which you feel that your boss may have no right to tell you what to do. Other times you may witness things that you feel very uncomfortable about. Should you hide your discomfort or should you take action? And what if taking action means personal risk?

The daily newspapers bring some of the more momentous of such cases to notoriety. Prominent businessmen have been sentenced to jail for taking illegal shortcuts at work. Employees have been fired for calling attention to unsavory practices. A working individual could find himself witness to, or in the midst of, behavior that he cannot condone. What is he or she to do? Where should we draw the line? What's right?

SHOULD I TELL?

QUESTION

I work for a large company. Frequently, when few people are around, I see my boss take merchandise out to his car. We have a comprehensive paperwork system, but none of these items has ever shown up in it. I once asked my boss if he wanted me to write up an item he was carrying out. He said, no, the company owed it to him. I am increasingly bothered by these incidents. Should I tell higher management about them?

QUESTION

I work in a small retail store. We have a new manager. On several occasions he has taken merchandise home, saying: "I am taking this home to see if my wife likes it. If she does, I'll bring in the money tomorrow." But he never does. He's also away from the store quite often, and we've been instructed to cover up his absences if the head office calls while he's away. What do you suggest we do?

QUESTION

I work for a small company; I handle accounts payable and the checkbook. The controller, my immediate supervisor, has asked me on several occasions to do some special accounting jobs for him. There always seems to be some discrepancy between the figures he gives me and the general ledger. I've asked him for an explanation a number of times, but he always avoids a direct answer. I feel very uncomfortable about these transactions, but I don't know enough about accounting to be *sure* that something is really wrong. Should I go to the president of the company with my concerns?

QUESTION

I work in a business that recently demoted a very competent manager and replaced him with another individual. Supposedly he was placed in this position because he has a specific background that the company needs.

As it turns out, this new man knows very little about this business. He is also a very heavy drinker—on the job, too. This has already interfered with his performance on the job. He has also told us never to say anything about all this to the owner of the business. I don't want to overstep my position; frankly, I fear the consequences, but the business cannot function if some action is not taken. What should I do?

QUESTION

I am employed as a plainclothes security officer; my duty is to detain shoplifters. I am concerned about my supervisor's drinking problem. Sometimes one can even smell alcohol on his breath when he arrives at work! Some of the other supervisors are good friends of his and seem inclined to cover up his habit.

If I report this man to higher authority, these others may take revenge on me and I may even get terminated. Can you suggest an alternative?

ANSWER

Each of you are caught on the horns of an ethical dilemma: You've identified a probable breach of ethics (and perhaps even of the law!) in your organizations, but to take action would quite likely place *you* in danger of reprisals from the accused party who, in all of these cases, is in a position of authority.

In trying to sort things out and work your way to the right course of action, I suggest a mental test. Picture yourself facing a group of people who are very important to you, whose opinion you value, and whose respect you seek. They could be your spouse, best friends, parents, children—or they could be a group of senior managers from your company. Now, imagine yourself having to account to these people for *your* conduct in response to these situations.

Suppose you don't take any action. Picture yourself explaining, in this imaginary scene, why you didn't. Do your explanations sound convincing? Or, do you cringe at the thought of having to justify shutting your eyes?

Nobody else can blithely tell you what to do in such situations. This mental test, however, might help you clarify your own thoughts and feelings and hold them up for comparison against the values you live by.

There really is no magical alternative to going to the owner or some other high-level manager and reporting a supervisor who steals or who has a drinking problem. (I shudder at the thought of the damage an alcoholic security supervisor can cause!) There is also no question that this will put you into significant jeopardy. While you can ask that your identity be kept confidential, you cannot count on it.

If you decide to take such action, seek out people in the organization who, by the nature of their jobs, are likely to take your complaints seriously. In a large organization, I would approach the internal audit group or the director of personnel; in a small one, the head of the company.

The choice is whether to undertake this risk by doing the right thing or hope to avoid the risk by keeping quiet. Only you can make this choice because it is you who will have to live with the consequences. And there can be negative consequences either way.

YOUR EMPLOYER WON'T GO TO JAIL FOR YOU

QUESTION

For the last four years I've worked for a company where it is a way of life to get the product out regardless, using whatever criteria necessary.

Some of my older and trusted employees assured me that our CEO was unaware of what was happening. Certainly some of the articles he wrote and speeches he gave convinced me of this also. Well, to make a long story short, I approached him on the mass cheating and illegal activities that were going on, and now I am out of a job.

How would you advise a member of middle management to handle pressures to perform illegal acts for the company?

ANSWER

I really respect you for what you did. No company should expect its employees to break the law on its behalf. When you go to work for a company, there should be a meeting of minds: You put your best effort and knowledge to work for the benefit of your employer in exchange for a salary. Breaking the law can never be part of this contract.

If you lose your job because of that attitude, you're probably better off in the long run. Remember, your employer will not go to jail for you.

BY REFUSING DRUGS, A MANAGER
COMMUNICATES POLICY

Managers carry an added burden: Because they are role models for others in the organization, all their actions are publicly scrutinized. When it involves ethics, the boss's behavior sets the rules for others.

QUESTION

I am a senior manager. I was recently invited to the home of one of my employees for a housewarming party. About thirty-five young professionals who work in my department were also present.

While I was there, I noticed a group gathered outside on the patio. I guess I'm naive, but I decided to go out and see if I could join the crowd. Well, they were smoking grass, and they had other drugs available. They were uncomfortable when they saw me but offered me some grass, which I declined.

I just didn't know what to do. In my panic, I instinctively refused, I am afraid, quite abruptly. I didn't want to alienate anyone, but I didn't want to indicate approval either. I don't use drugs myself, but I know that some of the people in my organization do. Am I being too conservative? No one has mentioned the incident, but this will probably be the last get-together I'll be invited to.

ANSWER

You absolutely did the right thing to decline, for at least two reasons. First, when in doubt, the best approach is to be true to yourself. You don't use drugs, so why should you change your behavior? The only reason you would have taken the grass was because of group pressure. You would have been very unhappy with yourself later, and you also would have lost your employees' respect.

The other reason is equally strong. While the party was private, many members of your department were present, so it clearly had strong ties to the workplace. Your conduct in that situation, whether you like it or not, is not just a private matter. Your reaction to the drug scene communicates company policy more strongly than a stack of memos.

Maybe you'll never get invited to another party, but your refusal to take drugs may give strength to others to stand on their own feet and say no to the goods offered next time. I think that's a good deal.

WOULD YOU TAKE A DRUG TEST IN ORDER TO GET PROMOTED?

Drugs, their presence, and ways of dealing with them have become a major issue at the workplace. *Drug testing* has emerged as a possible means of dealing with the problem, creating strong reactions pro and con, and a lot of soul-searching.

QUESTION

I have worked for one company a number of years. I have been hoping that I will be promoted to a supervisory position soon.

I've recently started to hear rumors that all supervisors will be required to submit to a drug test. I don't like this at all. I feel it is an invasion of my privacy. What I do outside of work should be my own business as long as I do the job I am expected to do and do it well. I am no longer sure I want to become a supervisor badly enough to agree to take this test. I also am concerned that if I back away from it, the assumption will be that I am a drug user, which I'm not.

I don't know what to do. Do you have any suggestions?

I solicited readers' views on this subject, even encouraging them to write anonymously. I received a flood of responses, surprisingly most of them fully signed!

READERS' RESPONSES

As an attorney specializing in wrongful-termination law, I believe that firing a good employee for refusing to take a drug test *should* be illegal. Unfortunately, the courts have not ruled on this issue yet and no one can tell if this practice will be found legal or not.

The drug-testing craze reminds me of the loyalty-oath crisis of the 1950s. Then people were forced out of jobs for refusing to sign oaths of allegiance, even though they were patriots and despite excellent work records. Now employees are forced to give urine samples even though they are not drug users and their work is good. Just as loyalty-oath requirements were eventually found to be illegal, so too, I believe, will drug testing of employees whose work performance is satisfactory be disapproved by the courts.

My recommendation to this employee: Start looking for another job. After you have found one, tell your manager how strongly you feel about drug testing—and that you want to work for an employer where performance is the only criterion for success.

• • •

People who object to drug testing complain about violation of their rights. What about the rights of employers? And what about the rights of fellow employees who do not use drugs? Frankly, I would welcome drug testing at the company where I work.

I see lack of productivity every day. I cannot say that it is all drug-related, but I do believe drug users are not productive. I feel that this is the big difference between the USA and Japan!

• • •

If an individual's drug use is so unnoticeable that the manager is not aware of it without resorting to a chemical test, is the employee's drug use really a work problem? Clearly it is not.

I feel that the true reasons why drug testing is advocated are not related to productivity and safety but to moral indignation. I don't feel that is a good enough reason to nullify people's civil rights.

These tests presume guilt and force a person to prove his innocence in a humiliating public display. I am completely opposed to drug testing in the workplace!

• • •

Taking drugs is against the law. It's a serious public problem and a source of lost productivity to business. While drug testing is fairly revolting and demeaning, I think a company is within its rights to protect itself.

• • •

I think people who submit to this indignity are to be applauded. They are helping to set an example. We don't object to breath tests for drunk drivers, and in recent times we have changed the image of heavy drinkers from macho to pitiful. I think we should do the same for drug users.

• • •

The notion of "invasion of privacy" is a distortion by the media and a vicious, contrived effort to belittle, smear, and discredit some very positive efforts by the Reagan administration to combat one of the most serious socioeconomic problems facing the country.

Society has a right to know about dope addiction in order to protect the safety and welfare of the majority.

As an entrepreneur and an employer, I would be one of the first to stand up for the rights of an employer to fire an employee for poor job performance. But how does the administration of drug testing tell me who is doing their job and who isn't?

• • •

As a former probation officer, I can only shake my head in puzzlement at all the silliness. I can perhaps see the point in very specific circumstances—an air-traffic controller who is suspected of use, for example. But for everyone else—do the proponents have any idea of what they are talking about?

For instance, do they intend to stand there and observe the sample being given to ensure that the well-known tricks of substituting "clean" urine are not employed? (And believe me, users are familiar with all the tricks.)

What a monumental waste of time, money, and energy on what could at best be a symbolic solution.

• • •

If the employee is clean, why not go along with it? The refusal gains nobody anything.

• • •

No drug testing at the workplace—unless nicotine and alcohol are included.

• • •

A serious problem is the inevitability of identifying nonusers as users. There are major questions about the accuracy of the tests, even if they are repeated. But even if the tests were 99 percent accurate—a very, very optimistic assumption—they would cause major problems. If the percentage of drug users in the employee population was low, say 5 percent, then simple arithmetic shows that for every five users we would falsely identify one nonuser as a user. This is clearly unacceptable.

• • •

From a toxicologist:

There is essentially *no* correlation between the presence of drugs in the urine and impairment from drug use at that time, as is the case with blood tests for alcohol level. Such absence of correlation represents a major limitation of urinary drug testing. One cannot answer the question of greatest concern: Was the individual impaired?

• • •

From a report by the American Occupational Medical Association, titled "Ethical Guidelines on Drug Screening in the Workplace":

Any requirement for screening for drugs should be based on reasonable business necessity. Such necessity might involve safety for the individual, other employees, or the public; security needs; requirements related to job performance; or requirements for a particular public image.

As I pored over the numerous responses from readers and the advice I received from associates, I had to think quite hard on the pros and cons of this issue. Frankly, I found myself changing sides several times.

Whenever I get too confused with an issue related to the question of what's right at the workplace, I like to go back to basics and remind myself that, first and foremost, a business must look after three groups of people: its customers, its employees, and its shareholders. Unless

222 One-on-One With Andy Grove

we can do well by these groups, we should not presume to undertake the righting of other wrongs.

I feel we must put stringent criteria on the use of drug testing at the workplace because it is likely to cause some serious, though unintended, consequences. One is the almost certain false accusations that statistically are bound to take place—with potentially harmful consequences to the careers of completely innocent individuals.

The other consequence is the probable polarization of employees. It is quite clear from the letters I received that people feel very strongly about this subject. Rightly or wrongly, they are committed to their viewpoints, and the introduction of broad testing would set employees against each other. Few businesses can afford such civil war–like conditions without hurting the three constituencies they are chartered to serve.

So, I ended up with these views. Drug testing at the workplace is justifiable under two circumstances: first, if there is a *probable cause* for suspecting that drugs were involved in causing poor performance, a mishap, or an accident on the job; and second, in cases that the American Occupational Medical Association calls "reasonable business necessity."

To make sure our criteria for drug testing an individual are rational, we might consider: Would we have subjected this person to a thorough physical exam in these same circumstances? If the answer is yes, then including drug testing can be justified. If not, our motivation is suspect.

Pilots, for instance, seem to meet the conditions of reasonable business necessity. They are also required to undergo periodic physicals. I see no reason against testing them, at the same time, for the presence of drugs. Future supervisors, on the other hand, are not usually required to take a physical before promotion. Consequently, I fail to see any logic in requiring them to submit to a drug test.

As to what the writer of the original letter, who posed the question, should do:

ANSWER

None of us can or should presume to advise you on such a truly personal decision. However, I hope that the views represented in these letters and my comments will help you clarify your thoughts so that you can arrive at a thoughtful decision that you can live with.

If you feel daring or comfortable enough to do so, *now* (before a policy is announced) is the time to go on record with how you feel about the prospect of being tested. Write a letter to the head of the company or the owner and explain how you feel about it and why. Your personal convictions could influence what will probably be an extremely close decision.

CATCH-22 AS THE COMPENSATION MANUAL

Some ethical issues are important enough that if you lose, you should leave your employer. If the very fabric of your organization lacks integrity, you should get out fast. In such a place, even if you win a particular skirmish, eventually you are destined to lose.

QUESTION

I've been working at a bank as a part-time new-accounts clerk. This position offers no benefits and minimal pay. Although in theory I'm a part-time employee, I've routinely been working forty-hour weeks. Also, since I had worked at this bank as a teller in the past, I'm often asked to work in that capacity at no extra pay. At such times I work next to brand-new tellers who make more money than I do.

I've talked to the personnel director about this situation, but he offered no help because the bank's policy doesn't allow the use of temporaries in teller positions!

Shouldn't I get benefits if I work a full forty-hour week? Should

I continue to do tellers' work without being paid as one? What should I do?

ANSWER

It seems to me that this bank is using temporary employees for a purpose quite different from smoothing their work load; it is using them as an underhanded way of reducing its payroll expenses. When the personnel manager refuses even to acknowledge the very existence of a policy violation that stares him in the face (in a manner that seems to have been lifted straight from *Catch-22*), I don't think you have much hope for a satisfactory resolution. The place sounds awful. I suggest you move on.

THE SARTORIAL BUCK STOPS WITH THE BOSS

Most issues of right and wrong are in the category of "Can they. . . ?" and "Should I. . . ?" Some requests or requirements the company places on you may be burdensome or objectionable but within the rational prerogative of an employer, while others are not. How do you determine which? Consider each situation with as much common sense and objectivity as you can muster.

QUESTION

I work as an usher at a theater. Recently I got a new, fashionable haircut—different but not in bad taste at all. My boss didn't like it and suspended me for two weeks. Is it right for a manager to dictate his employee's hairstyle?

ANSWER

Your boss is responsible for presenting to the public (his customers) a group of employees who are dressed and groomed in such a way that, at a minimum, they don't repel those who ultimately pay all your salaries.

So, yes, it is right for him to be concerned with all aspects of your appearance. He may not always be *right* in deciding what is or is not appropriate, just as he is probably not always right in his choice of shows—but it has to be his call.

GETTING OD'D ON BUSINESS DINNERS . . .

QUESTION

I work in sales for a small company. Part of my job is entertaining clients. I spend several nights a week taking various clients to dinner.

Recently my boss, the owner of the company, has asked me to attend a variety of social functions, such as the meetings of professional groups, all in the evening. None of these has anything to do with our business. My boss maintains that I am likely to make contacts that might be useful at some time, saying, "You can never tell."

I think these events are a needless imposition on my personal time. Who is right?

ANSWER

Neither you nor your boss is automatically right or wrong. Let me suggest a framework that might enable the two of you to decide rationally what to do.

First, you should agree on how many evenings a week you can be expected to spend on business-related entertainment. After you have agreed on a number, the next question is how to use these evenings to the best advantage. You and your boss should decide together whether it's more useful to take certain clients to dinner or to go to one of the social functions you refer to, and develop some guidelines for choosing one or the other.

The point is, while all of these activities have some usefulness, none is likely to be crucial. You and your boss need to decide which will benefit your business most. Telling you to do both is just an attempt to avoid making necessary choices.

SHE'S A COMPANY SECRETARY, NOT A PERSONAL ONE

QUESTION

I am a manager of a department of engineers, and I have a secretary who supports me and my group. I'm also single. I have certain personal tasks that I assign to my secretary, such as picking up my laundry while she's out at lunch and balancing my checkbook, which suffers a lot of neglect.

I let her do these jobs on company time, so frankly, I don't understand why I get so much resistance. She claims that it's just not part of her job. I don't see that she has any reason to complain. Am I right or wrong?

ANSWER

Unless your secretary was hired specifically to do personal services for you as a company-paid benefit, you are embarking on a very dangerous path. Although it's possible to interpret any personal service she might render to you as ultimately benefiting the company, you must draw the line someplace. The question is where. I suggest the following criterion:

If the work she performs contributes *directly* to the business of your employer, it's OK. So, typing your business correspondence, taking and sending messages for you, and even bringing coffee for business meetings are all proper parts of the job. But fetching your laundry, balancing your checkbook, or arranging your personal dinner parties are services rendered to you as an individual.

Using your secretary this way is no different than misappropriating a company asset for personal use. Some might argue that taking the company truck home to do house chores, or taking stationery from the company's storeroom for personal use are somehow indirectly helping the company. These are dangerous and flimsy rationalizations.

In my view, your secretary's opposition to rendering personal services is well-founded.

I'M AFRAID TO SAY NO

Of course, knowing what is right and doing it—going to the wall, if necessary—are two different things.

QUESTION

I read your column about the guy who expects his secretary to pick up his laundry and balance his checkbook. I'm a facilities maintenance tech. My department takes care of the maintenance needs of the company. One of the department managers called me aside the other day and told me that he wants me to help him out with a construction problem he's having.

I feel manipulated and tremendously pressured. He's a high-level guy; I'm afraid of him. What if I tell him no and he makes it a point to go after me? What should I say?

ANSWER

It's absolutely wrong for your boss to pressure you into doing personal services for him. Still, I hesitate to advise you to refuse his demand. The tone of your letter makes me feel that you may be in real jeopardy. What you do about your problem depends on how much risk you can take.

Try to find an ally in the personnel department who will listen to your problem on a confidential basis. His or her involvement may protect you if you are later persecuted by this manager.

While we may disapprove of some practices at the workplace, not all of them are causes for major upheavals. Sometimes acceptance of a practice you dislike or disagree with is a far more appropriate course of action than raising a hue and cry over it. Here are a couple of examples.

BAD MANNERS DON'T WARRANT HUGE OPPOSITION

QUESTION

Something petty bothers me. Whenever my boss calls me on the phone, he has the call placed by his secretary, and he only gets on the line after I am already on the phone. I can't find anything terribly wrong with this, but it irritates me anyway. Is this a proper practice?

ANSWER

I have to admit to a lifelong irritation over this practice myself, and I think there *is* something basically wrong with it. Whenever another person has a call placed by a secretary, he makes a statement to the effect that his time is more valuable than yours: It's OK for you to wait on the line for him, but it would be wasteful for him to wait for you. Of course, it's entirely possible that another individual's time is more valuable than yours, but a blatant reminder is simply tacky.

Still, it's not a huge matter. It's no worse than someone walking out the door ahead of you without hesitation. It's impolite but hardly worth making a fuss over. So, while I agree with your feelings on the matter, I suggest that you just shrug them off.

LET SLEEPING DOGS LIE—BUT ONLY AFTER YOU GET YOUR ANSWER

QUESTION

I work in the shipping and receiving area of an electronics company. I have a new supervisor. He's a pretty decent guy; the only problem is, he falls asleep in the storeroom almost every day for about an hour.

From time to time, some things need to be done that I'm not sure how to do. Should I wake him, or tell his boss about him—or just let sleeping dogs lie?

ANSWER

I don't think you need to report him; the situation doesn't represent an emergency. In time, his manager will find out about your boss's habit and deal with it. If you need your supervisor, just wake him up, matter-of-factly and without apologies. He's paid to do his job, so call on him to do it whenever it's necessary.

20

Be Leery of Fads and Stereotypes

YOU and I traveled a long road together, with the workplace as our landscape. We dealt with problems that people encounter there—with each other, with their bosses, with their employees. The principle that *common sense* and *straight dealing* usually lead to the right answer was our compass.

A word of warning is in order here. The field of managing is filled with myths and fads to an unusually high degree. During the twenty years that I have been a manager, many buzzwords and panaceas appeared, eclipsed, and disappeared, only to be replaced by new ones. Management by objectives, active listening, matrix management, quality circles, participatory management, theory X/theory Y, various American fantasies of Japanese management style—all were meant to make work go better, and each contained some wisdom. But all too often we want to use them as ready-made templates instead of thinking our way through a problem and coming up with our own answer.

Examples abound of well-intended clichés that, taken out of the proper perspective, mislead. One of the current slogans is that we need to heed our customers more closely. Now, nobody can take issue with that. But *who* is the customer? The automatic interpretation points to those who buy the firm's products or services. But what if you run an administrative group and you *never* see the firm's customers? Should you drop processing purchase orders and go on a field trip, knocking on customers' doors?

Common sense suggests that there are better things for you to do. No matter what work you do, you have customers of your own—but often they are internal ones: people who depend on your work so they can do theirs. Understanding *their* needs, problems, and satisfaction level is what you need to work on instead of traipsing around the country.

The point is, the advice to pay more attention to the needs of the customer is sound. But you can't leave it at that. You must think through what this means to you in your particular situation. Otherwise you are likely to spin your wheels and waste your time and that of others.

SUPERSTARS

Another example. We all know that a relatively small portion of the work force is often responsible for a disproportionate share of results and achievements. It then follows that every business must take good care of these individuals—our "superstars." But we also know that most organizations could improve their performance substantially by improving the *teamwork* between their employees. One cliché is in conflict with the other: Catering too much to a small minority is likely to cause resentment in the rest of the workers, and that will hinder collaboration.

Put another way, one of the most important recent advances in the working world has been the gradual lessening of class distinctions. If we treat our superstars too differently from other employees, we may end up creating a new class distinction in place of the old one—and teamwork will suffer.

QUESTION

What is the best way to manage "superstars"? Should I make allowances and treat them differently than other employees?

ANSWER

Only to this extent: Put the superstars to work on projects where their talents will have the greatest potential impact on the company. Spend your time with them to get familiar with the details of their work and give them as much feedback as you are capable of. Also, compensate them according to their contributions—but *do not* treat them as a privileged class.

In other words, push them harder? Yes. Pay them more? By all means. Give them reserved parking spaces? No!

Currently, entrepreneurship is *in*. It's credited with much of the good that has taken place in the U.S. economy, and rightly so. As often happens, though, we've gone overboard in celebrating entrepreneurs, the creators of new ideas. We forget that progress is just as dependent on exe*cutors* and *implementers,* people who can bring the good ideas to fruition. While we put the entrepreneur on a pedestal, it's important that we place the implementer on a pedestal of equal height and glory!

How? By praising and publicizing the implementer's contributions along with those of the entrepreneur, and by rewarding both individuals equally. We must keep in mind that every idea is only as good as the tangible, measurable results it brings forth.

It's also fashionable these days to talk a great deal about *corporate cultures*. Far be it from me to minimize their importance! A strong corporate culture is the invisible hand that guides how things are done in an organization. The phrase, "You just can't do that here," is extremely powerful, more so than any written rules or policy manuals. I also think that our recent enhanced awareness of the power and importance of corporate cultures is a useful development, but the naïveté with which people think of them is unfortunate. "Our culture is not right; we must change it" is a phrase often heard today. As if it was anywhere near that simple!

MIDDLE MANAGEMENT IS THE KEY TO CORPORATE CHANGE

QUESTION

I work for a large company. We had a recent management shake-up and now have a new president. A few weeks after he arrived he sent a memo to all employees saying that most of our problems are caused by lack of cooperation and teamwork among the employees. He promised to change our culture to eliminate this and to enable us to work more closely with each other.

Can this be done? I'm a bit skeptical.

ANSWER

It depends on your president's approach. It is very difficult to accomplish a change like this throughout the company hierarchy. A large organization has many layers of management, and bringing about a change in culture—that is, a lasting change in values and preferences—through these layers without distortion is practically impossible.

Organizational cultures are easy to establish when a business is young. I remember reading about President Carter's attempt to introduce the idea of "management by objectives" into the federal government. Evidently, it didn't work too well. For the government to be practicing management by objectives properly, the practice should have been started by George Washington.

To change the way an entire organization operates, all middle managers in that organization must be enlisted as *agents of change*. This can only be done if top management communicates *directly* and *in depth* with a large number of middle managers. This is a very difficult and time-consuming task, but there is just no shortcut or substitute for it.

Middle managers *are* capable of changing their immediate environment. It is small enough and sufficiently accessible that changes can be introduced quite rapidly. For example, a manager can introduce the practice of management by objectives into his own group or department with relative ease. Likewise, he can change the style of meetings or decision making among the people whom he directly supervises.

So, if your president is to make any lasting difference in regard to the degree of cooperativeness within the company, he would need to dedicate himself to working with your company's middle management. He would need to meet with them in their own environment, see firsthand how they operate, and exert his influence on their approach. Then, over time, these middle managers would change their approach and spread the new style to their own groups, as so many disciples. This may be a long and laborious process, but it is the only way corporate styles and cultures can be changed.

I'd like to end with . . .

FIVE KEY PRINCIPLES

This book started with the boss who constantly belittled his employee and worked its way to corporate cultures. As I look back and reflect, a few key principles stand out. Follow them!

FIRST—and this is very important—enjoy your work. It's impossible to like all of it. Sometimes you'll chafe under its unrelenting nature, other times you'll be bored, but overall you must enjoy it. I am convinced that most people will like their work if they can see that what they do makes a difference and if they approach their work with a bit of zest, maybe even playfulness. Doing so introduces a bit of levity when it's most needed and leads to camaraderie.

SECOND, be totally dedicated to the substance of your work, to the end result, the output; not *how* you got to it or whose idea it was or whether you look good or not.

THIRD, respect the work of all those who respect their own work, from vice presidents to sales clerks, from maintenance technicians to security officers. Nobody is unimportant: It takes all levels and all jobs to run a functioning organization.

FOURTH, be straight with everyone. I hate it when people are not honest with me, and I would hate myself if I weren't straight with them. This isn't an easy principle to stick to. There are always many reasons (better to call them excuses) to compromise a little here or there. We may reason that people are not ready to hear the truth or the bad news, that the time isn't right, or whatever. Giving in to those tempting rationalizations usually leads to conduct that can be ethically wrong and will backfire every time.

And, ALWAYS, when stumped, stop and *think* your way through to *your own* answers!

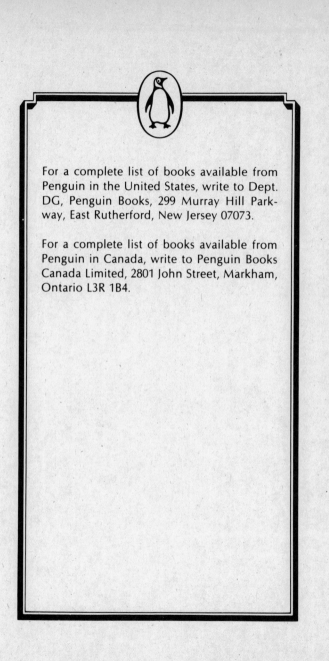

For a complete list of books available from Penguin in the United States, write to Dept. DG, Penguin Books, 299 Murray Hill Parkway, East Rutherford, New Jersey 07073.

For a complete list of books available from Penguin in Canada, write to Penguin Books Canada Limited, 2801 John Street, Markham, Ontario L3R 1B4.